Higher Levels of Success

You're Going To Need This!

By Lona Richard

Copyright © 2011 by Lona Richard

Higher Levels of Success
by Lona Richard

Printed in the United States of America

ISBN 9781607916956

All rights reserved solely by the author. The author guarantees all contents are original and do not infringe upon the legal rights of any other person or work. No part of this book may be reproduced in any form without the permission of the author. The views expressed in this book are not necessarily those of the publisher.

Unless otherwise indicated, Bible quotations are taken from The King James Version of the Bible; The Holy Bible, New International Version (NIV). Copyright © 1973, 1978, 1984 by International Bible Society. Used by permission of Zondervan Bible Publishers; and The Message. Copyright © 1993, 1994, 1995, 1996, 2000, 2001, 2002 by NavPress Publishing Group. Used by permission.

Cover photo by Josh Tumlin, Guardian Photography

www.xulonpress.com

Acknowledgments

With special thanks:

To my parents, Joseph and Rose Richard, for instilling in me the beginning of a lifelong relationship and supernatural journey with my Lord and Savior, Jesus Christ. They taught me honesty, integrity, and insisted that I maintain a character held to a higher standard than the world condones—the standard of God's word.

Introduction

Every day is new territory to be conquered. No looking back. No going back. New levels. You must have New dimensional thinking if you are going to have New dimensional living. You must have New dimensional anointing (ability and enablement of God) to serve Him and to accomplish what He wants done. You also MUST HAVE the grace to do ALL that God has called you to do, to be effective, to constantly and consistently move forward. The Holy Spirit enables and assists us in hearing clearly from God and understanding clearly what it is we need to do next and how to go about it.

God will promote you in spite of the opinions of men.

Most men and women chase after money, material things, fame, glamour...as well as other men and other women. If they would only seek (chase after) God, then all those other things would begin to chase after them!

The reason you are not successful is because you are relying on your own thoughts.

Isaiah 55:8-11 *For my thoughts are not your thoughts, neither are your ways my ways, saith the Lord. 9) For as the heavens are higher than the earth, so are my ways higher than your ways, and my thoughts than your thoughts. 10)*

For as the rain cometh down, and the snow from heaven, and returneth not thither, but watereth the earth, and maketh it bring forth and bud, that it may give seed to the sower, and bread to the eater: 11) So shall my word be that goeth forth out of my mouth: it shall not return unto me void, but it shall accomplish that which I please, and it shall prosper in the thing whereto I sent it.

God petitioned me to write this book, just as he instructed Habakkuk. **Habakkuk 2:2-3** *Then the Lord replied: "Write down the revelation and make it plain on tablets so that a herald (those that read it and receive it) may <u>run with it</u>. For the revelation awaits an appointed time; it speaks of the end and <u>will not prove false</u>. <u>Though it linger, wait for it</u>; it will certainly come and not delay.*

As you plunge into the pages that follow, God will surely reveal to you different areas of your life that require adjustment to succeed. With each change and adjustment you make, you cross over into new levels of success, and advance toward your destiny. Regardless of whether you are applying the nuggets and principals that follow to your business or your personal and family relationships, success and a better life WILL manifest.

Table of Contents

Acknowledgements iii
Introduction v

Part One: <u>Identifying Enemies to Success</u> 11
Ten Reasons (Things) That Cause People / Businesses to Fail

    1. Procrastination 13
    2. Not Enough Prayer 18
    3. Wrong Associations 25
    4. Negative Thinking 29
    5. Murmuring and Complaining 34
    6. Not Spending Time & Money Wisely 41
    7. Arrogance or Haughtiness 53
    8. Lack of Planning 59
    9. Instability 67
    10. Greed 75

Part Two: <u>Positioning Yourself for Success</u> 79

    11. Position For Transition (Increase) 81
    12. Get Ready For the Transfer of Wealth 86
    13. We Have Everything We Need to Fulfill Our Destiny 89

14. You Have the Anointing 95
15. Use the Resources He Has Given You 97
16. Focused Commitment to the Vision 100
17. New Levels of Success Require New
    Levels of Commitment 106
18. New Levels of Success Require Increased
    Responsibility 109
19. Positioned, Streamlined, Ready For
    the Race 112

Part Three: <u>Warding Off Hindrances</u> 115
Holding On To Your Success

20. Take Off The Limitations 117
21. Get the "H" Out of Here 121
22. The Catastrophic "C's" 125
23. The Deadly "D's" 132
24. Spirit of Excellence 164

Part Four: <u>Living The Best You've Ever Lived</u> 171
R...I...P Away Your Limitations, Experience
Higher Levels of Success!

25. Resist 173
26. Insist 182
27. Persist 190

Part One

Identifying Enemies To Success
Ten Reasons (Things) That Cause People/Businesses To Fail

Chapter 1

Procrastination

I've got so much to do. This can wait until tomorrow. Why can't they get someone else to do this. It seems like they've got me doing everything. Don't they understand I've already got all this other stuff going on?

Sound familiar? Have you ever said any of these statements to yourself or those around you? Certainly, when a deadline or date/time of commitment and responsibility comes due, we should have planned ahead or done it way ahead of time. Sometimes we have input on when things come due, but there are times when unexpected things will come up, actions required on our part come up and must be dealt with NOW—before we can do even one more thing. We must remain flexible. We must keep our priorities straight. We must plan ahead. We must DO those things today that absolutely need to be done today.

Procrastination is putting off doing something that needs to be or can be done right now—until later. Dictionary.com defines [1]procrastination – 1) to defer action; 2) delay; 3) put off until another day or time. Deadlines, commitments, opportunities, character and integrity are lost (gone—

some forever) because of procrastination. Deadlines are not met. Jobs and contracts are lost. Industry calls it "good faith effort". People who put their faith and trust in you to take care of something you said you would do—but didn't. Now they don't trust you anymore. They can't take you at your word anymore. The trust / dependability factor has been broken. Sometimes that takes years to restore, if ever. When businesses and people place their trust in you to do something when you said you would do it, they depend that you will take care of that job, detail, care of a situation/person the way it needs to be done in order to get a certain effect or result accomplished.

<u>Proverbs 6:10-11</u> *Yet a little sleep, a little slumber, a little folding of the hands to sleep (rest): 11) So shall thy poverty come as one (a prowler) that travelleth, and thy want (need) as an armed man.*

In order to get the job done, in order to make progress, in order to be stable, in order to move forward, in order to succeed, you need to remove procrastination from your life. Procrastination must be totally removed from your habits, and removed from your thinking that it is okay to put things off. Procrastination is as much of a burglar as the thief of distraction and deception. We must identify and recognize it as an ensnarement that causes people to fail in order to diligently avoid it. Procrastination causes businesses and people to fail. Procrastination minimizes effectiveness. Procrastination delays us—and in some cases STOPS us from reaching our destiny. The graveyard is full of people who never attained their goals, never fulfilled their dreams—because they gave in to procrastination.

Higher Levels of Success

Take a quiet moment to review, assess and think about the last 24 hours, and the last week of your life. How was your time spent?

_____

_____

How many times did you get caught up in things: a conversation, a television show, a magazine, said "Yes" to an outing with friends/relatives—when you really should have been studying, reading the Word, working in your yard, cleaning your car, repairing a minor repair/leak, so it didn't turn into a major one? Did you get caught up in a conversation that took you off schedule by 30 minutes or more?

_____

_____

Did you get caught up in your own or someone else's turmoil, drama, saga of THEIR OWN PROCRASTINATION—and either it sucked (drained) the energy out of you and/or took up more of your day than you had to give?

_____

_____

What areas of your business, church, family time, finances, physical fitness, eating properly, maintenance of your home and car have you been putting off (procrastinating) doing? List them in the space provided below.

Business
_____

Relationship With God
_____

Family Time
_____

Finances
_____

Physical Fitness
_____

Eating Properly
_____

Maintenance of Home/Apartment
_____

Maintenance of Auto

    Procrastination is so subtle that it creeps into our lives mentally, physically, emotionally, financially, socially, and spiritually. We have all been guilty of it. The sad truth is that once you give in to procrastination, the more you find it easy to put things off on a daily basis. The harder cases get labeled. But every day, we need to stay aware, alert, and adamant about doing what needs to be done This Day! Procrastination inhibits, cheats, cuts short, and aborts completion of accomplishments, goals, and dreams. The consequences and results of procrastination are as deadly and destructive as any addiction—alcohol, drugs, gambling, shopping, overspending (only to name a few). However, procrastination never seems to receive the proper credit and recognition that it truly deserves.

Right now, I pray that those reading this book make a daily effort and determination to eradicate procrastination from every area of their lives from this day forward in Jesus' name.

Chapter 2

Not Enough Prayer

Rushing off to the office, rushing off to the job, rushing to get the children to school, rushing to soccer-gymnastics-dance-sports-karate practice/event, rushing to the fitness club, rushing off to the grocery store, rushing to get home and get supper on the table, rushing to get homework done and projects completed, rushing to get the children ready for bed. In every given 24-hour period, we rush from one commitment, responsibility, and deadline to the next.

Each day—each 24-hour period, needs to not only begin with prayer and getting started with God, seeking God's wisdom and protection for a new day, and commanding each new day to manifest only God's best; but prayer is where we invite God into every situation, relationship, occasion, and opportunity—before it becomes a problem. Why wouldn't we take the time to invite God (who knows all and succeeds in everything He does and is a part of) to give us guidance, direction, insight and instruction into every detail and need that affects our business, our family and loved ones, and our personal needs?

Prayer opens the door for God to move in our lives and in our situations. When we pray, we invite God to move on the situations in our lives. We NEED His guidance, direction, instruction AND intervention.

When are you supposed to pray? **1Thessalonians 5:17-18** *Pray without ceasing. 19) In every thing give thanks: for this is the will of God in Christ Jesus concerning you.*

We are to begin our day with prayer. In doing so, we put God first and dedicate the work and accomplishments of that day to Him. We are to pray to him in ALL things continually throughout the day, and in doing so, include Him in everything as our day unfolds and continues to nightfall and even before we put our heads on the pillow to sleep and commit our rest unto Him. **Matthew 6:33** *But seek ye first the kingdom (God's ways and His thoughts on every matter), and His righteousness; and all these things shall be added unto you.* When we seek God FIRST, and commit everything that pertains to us (placing them in His most capable hands FIRST), then He takes care of us, making sure that all things are working out for our good. **Romans 8:28** *And we know that ALL things work together for good to them that love God, to them who are the called according to His purpose.*

Proverbs 3:5 *Trust in the Lord with ALL thine heart; and lean not unto thine own understanding. 6) In all thy ways acknowledge Him, and He shall direct (make smooth and straight) thy paths.* When we put our daily work, efforts, needs before God FIRST—not after we tried it on our own and made a mess of things; God blesses that order. God sees our obedience to Proverbs 3:5. This is the way we are to do things. The one living and true God who knows exactly what it will take to succeed and manifest the best for each one of us, makes it happen for our good. He sees to it that we are taken care of. He orchestrates and moves into place at the proper time, the resources (necessary people, material—supplies and finances) He has put at our disposal to get those things done that He predestined us to do (on a daily basis). Just like He did for Moses, David, Joseph—just to name a few in the Bible. He is still doing it today—if we just put Him FIRST, and daily put it in His hands FIRST thing each day. When we take time to pray, we seek the Lord about our decisions, that is what keeps us stable and successful—even when opposition comes against us in business or in our personal lives, we stand on the word of God, and also stand on what we heard God speak to us during our time spent in His presence.

We also pray for favor with God and with man both in our business transactions and personal life transactions and daily work and occurrences. **Proverbs 3:4** *So shalt thou find favour and good understanding in the sight of God and man.* **Psalms 5:12** *For thou, Lord, wilt bless the righteous (those who obey the scriptures); with favour wilt thou compass (surround) him as with a shield.* Parents are to pray for God's favor daily for their children and grandchildren. 1 Samuel 2:26 *And the child Samuel grew on, and was in favour both with the Lord, and also with men.*

What if you have already prayed and not yet seen the answers to your prayers manifest (happen). God heard you the FIRST time. What you are to do is continue to thank Him daily for answering that prayer and working it out to your advantage. God's word is working (day and night) and God is working this situation or problem out for you—even if it doesn't "appear" that anything is happening. **John 14:14** *If ye shall ask any thing in my name, I will do it.* Our part is to believe, and thank Him. It SHALL come to pass—if only we believe (trust Him to do what He says He will do).

When You Pray, You MUST ...
1. Pray according to the scripture that applies to your situation.
2. Believe that God will do what He said He would do.
3. Expect God to Move on Your Behalf.
4. See Yourself Already Having the Problem Solved, Need Met, Obstacle Overcome, Goal Attained, Project Completed, Degree and Associated Career in Place, the Success/Wholeness/Dreams Fulfilled Results that You Prayed For (Desired).

<u>PRAYER GETS RESULTS when 2 requirements are met</u>:
1) The request MUST line up with the Word (have scripture applied to it). This assures that we are praying in line with God's will (God's Word or scripture is His will). **<u>1 John 5:14-15</u>** *And this is the confidence that we have in Him, that, if we ask ANY THING according to His will, He heareth us: 15) And if we know that He hears us, WHATSOEVER we ask, we know that we have the petitions that we desired (asked) of Him.*
2) The person praying MUST believe he receives what he is asking for at the moment he finishes the prayer with "in Jesus' name, I pray".

<u>Isaiah 55:11</u> *So shall My word be that goeth forth out of my mouth: it shall NOT RETURN UNTO ME VOID, but it shall accomplish that which I please, and it shall prosper (accomplish, succeed) in the thing whereto I sent* *it*. Because God said His word would not go void, and without faith it is impossible to please God (cause Him to move and intervene on our behalf).

Hebrews 11:6 *But without faith it is impossible to please Him: for he that cometh to God (prays) MUST believe that He is, and that He is a rewarder of them that diligently seek Him.*

Think for a moment. What steps it will take to Get Your Problem Solved?

_____

_____

What steps will it take to Get Your Need Met?

_____

_____

What steps will it take to Overcome the Obstacle You are Facing?

_____

_____

What steps will it take to Attain Your Goal(s)?

_____

_____

What steps will it take to Complete Your Project?

_____

_____

What steps will it take to Get Your Degree and Make the Associated Career Change a Reality in Your Life?

_____

_____

What steps will it take to make what you view as True Success in your life happen?

_____

_____

What steps will it take to bring consistent Wholeness in your Life?

_____

_____

List your Dreams.

_____

_____

What are the steps needed to bring these Dreams to Fulfillment?

_____

_____

_____

_____

Chapter 3

Wrong Associations

Psalms 1:1 *Blessed (empowered to prosper, certain to succeed) is the man that walketh not in the counsel of the ungodly, nor standeth in the way of sinners, nor sitteth in the seat of the scornful.*

What Have You Opened Yourself Up To?

What friendships, commitments (things that take up your time), responsibilities or habits have you gotten yourself into (either by volunteering, agreeing to help someone do something, or habits) that are not going to assist you in moving forward in attaining your goal, degree, career, promotion, new home, smaller clothing size (health habits), more structure, more organized, and no procrastinations? What drama, and whose drama sucked you into total stagnation, uselessness and unproductive hours—right along with the one using their mouth and their time carrying on and on with the gossip, the opinionated comments, accusations and d-r-a-m-a? Ever notice how people who have drama in their lives tend to want to try and suck you into their drama? You end up being as unproductive and unsuccessful as they are.

It is assessment time. Make a list of how you spend your time in a given week. Yes...take a sheet of paper, turn it sideways, and section it off into Sunday-Saturday like a calendar does—only you will list what you did last week from the time you got up that morning until the time you went to sleep that night. Now review if your time was spent doing things that helped you move toward your goal, or took you off track and away from getting there more quickly.

You need to start spending your time wisely, so that your 3-day journey doesn't turn into the 40-year wilderness wandering about in meaningless existence. Who wants to "share" that? People who are really your friends will want you to be ALL God intended you to be ALL the time.

Do Not Partner With Them

(Ephesians 5:6-7) *Let no one deceive you with empty words, for because of such things God's wrath comes on those who are disobedient. Therefore do not be partners with them.*

Here, God clearly tells us not only to be obedient; He also tells us the consequences of disobedience. He also commands us not to partner (have no part) with those who consistently, knowingly disobey Him. We are born with success in us. We are made by a Creator who cannot fail. We have been formed in the likeness and image of Him. We are designed to succeed. Therefore, if success is not a constant part and result of our work and efforts, then we are doing something outside of the will of God. There is disobedience going on somewhere in some area of our lives.

As my children were growing up, I always told them, "You wouldn't take financial advice from someone who is bankrupt—would you?" "If you are going to take advice from someone, make sure it is Godly counsel from someone that is successful".

Wrong associations—we cannot continue to maintain relationships with people who speak against the word of God. The negative words and unbelief that they insist on practicing will eventually impact the way we think, the things we do, and our success in life. This applies to business owners, as well as marriages, and personal relationships.

2 Corinthians 6:14 *Be ye not unequally yoked together with unbelievers: for what fellowship hath righteousness with unrighteousness? And what communion hath light with darkness?*

What friendships and relationships came to mind when you read the section on "Wrong Associations"? List their names here.

_____

_____

Think about when you are with these friends and acquaintances—maybe even family members. After spending time with them do you come away feeling discouraged?
_____Yes _____No

Do they encourage, build you up and inspire you to be your best and do your best? _____ Yes _____ No

You should spend time with those who encourage and inspire you. You should spend time with those who push you toward your goals, toward greater accomplishments and higher levels of success—not those who would try to talk you out of doing what it takes to have a better life, more success in your life, and reaching your destiny. If those you spend time with become a limitation, instead of helping you overcome your limitations, you need to limit your time with them.

Pray this Prayer: Lord Jesus, surround me with godly counsel and wisdom at all times. Cause the friends and people who speak into my hearing to speak only things that will encourage me, build me up and cause me to attain higher levels of success in my life, in Jesus' name. Please help me to see which of my friends are helping me reach my goals, and which of my friends don't want to see me get ahead, because it will show them up too badly. Then, help me to make adjustments to leave those alone that aren't helping me move forward with my life and my goals, in Jesus' name.

Chapter 4

Negative Thinking

Proverbs 23:7 *For as he thinketh in his heart, so is he:*

God wants us to come up to a higher level of thinking. We can only behave (do) as highly or successfully as we think (dwell on, operate in). As long as we dwell on and insist on operating only within the deadlines, time frames and accomplishments that the world gives and assigns to us, then we will have frustration. It will leave us feeling frustrated, worn out, and overwhelmed. The higher level of thinking brings us to dwell on the things that God wants us to think about. He is looking at and seeing things on a much, MUCH, higher level; much, MUCH higher elevation; much, MUCH higher standard than the world will EVER have or make available to us.

As we rise to a higher level of thinking, we rise to a higher level of being.

We are no longer held down (bound) to the limitations, the deadlines, the mundane accomplishments and rewards of this world. The rewards God has promised to us are MORE than we could ever ask or imagine. We rise to the higher level when we maintain the higher level of thinking God wants us to have. Consistently insisting on the higher level of thinking, the higher level of living, the higher level of attainment and accomplishments, the higher level (come up higher) of spiritual understanding, the higher level of understanding of the Word (the perfect will of God for us) and the higher level of spiritual and prayerful effectiveness (spiritually, physically, mentally, emotionally, and financially).

As children of God, we are not of this world, so we should not limit ourselves in the thinking, the deadlines, the accomplishments, the understanding of this world. We are the sons and daughters of the Most High God, so we should think on a Higher Level, and BE on a Higher Level, so we can get closer and closer to our Daddy God. We operate and conduct our lives according to His standards, according to the ability He has given us, and according to the wisdom He downloads to us each day as we ask and seek Him to download it.

We ask the Holy Spirit daily (every 24-hour period) to show us (help us to see, hear and obey) the voice of God and show us what He would have us to do and how we are to go about it. Only by His direction, instruction and consistently and continuously showing us can we continue going higher and higher in Christ, in our spiritual understanding, in our walk with God, in our relationship with God (building our relationship and going Higher and Higher in Christ spiritually).

When you obey and do those things that the Holy Spirit shows you need to be done, God does two things: 1) He causes you to be effective in every situation that you put your hand to; and 2) He takes care of everything else in your life—your children, your job (your business), your finances, and your family.

You see, as you go Higher and aspire (desire) to go Higher and understand the things of Christ, God reveals things to you that you would otherwise have not ever seen (and understood) about the situations in your life and about Him. <u>These things are only revealed to those who aspire (sincerely desire) to go UP in Christ</u>. **Jeremiah 33:3** *Call unto me and I will answer you and I will show you great and unsearchable things that you do not know.*

The Holy Spirit has been sent to us to assist (help) us to hear and understand the voice and the vision (understanding) that God gives us and speaks to us every time we make ourselves available to Him. He helps us to hear and see what He is telling or showing us. We certainly don't utilize the precious Holy Spirit's Divine assistance as MUCH as we need to. We should be reaping ALL the Benefits God has available for us.

Joshua 1:8 *This book of the law shall not depart out of thy mouth; but thou shall <u>meditate</u> on it day and night.*

Think about it. This is a commandment from God. Have you passed right by it and ignored it? What have you been spending your time "thinking on" or about?

_____

_____

Is there a recording that has been playing past arguments, gossip, accusations, drama, or even images in a television show that are not wholesome, or good for you? Do these recordings/images get you off into some bad, negative thoughts you should not be allowing to continue to go on in your head?

_____

_____

Do these thoughts cause you to be encouraged and upbeat or discouraged, angry, and depressed?

_____

_____

Do these thoughts cause you to feel insignificant about yourself or your work? Do you feel that someone has made you feel small or "less than" in your self-worth, or true value and contribution you know you bring to the workplace or relationship?

_____

_____

    Right now, we ask God to help us forgive them for anything that was said or done. We release them, so we can get past this thing that took place, and insist on getting on with our lives in a progressive and successful pace and manner in Jesus' name.

    2 Corinthians 10:5 *Casting down imaginations, and every high thing that exalteth itself against the knowledge* *of God, and bringing into captivity every thought to the obedience of Christ;*

Personalize this time and use it to reflect on your thinking. You need to <u>spend your time thinking only on positive things</u>, so that we stay focused, stay positive, stay progressive and successful. If anything that doesn't line up with the word of God pops into your mind, kick it out. Say, "That's not my thought. The blood of Jesus covers my thoughts in Jesus' name". That's how you kick out negative (unproductive, unfruitful, unsuccessful) thoughts and bring your thoughts into the obedience of Christ.

Joshua 1:8 *This book of the law (Bible, God's Word) shall not depart out of thy mouth; but thou shalt meditate (think, ponder) therein day and night, that thou mayest observe to do according to all that is written therein: <u>for then thou shalt make thy way prosperous, and then thou shalt have good success.</u>*

Chapter 5

Murmuring and Complaining

John 5:43 *Jesus therefore answered and said unto them, "Murmur not amongst yourselves". (Stop grumbling).*

Murmuring and complaining only drains your energy and stops you from getting the most out of your workday or time spent with loved ones. Murmuring and complaining sows discord, stifles creativity and progress, and accomplishes nothing. Murmuring and complaining causes discouragement, negativity, and complacency and often leads to rebellion. "Why bother" attitudes often follow murmuring and complaining. "Murmuring and complaining" like to get other people to do the same, so they can feel better about having a bad attitude about a situation. Bad-mouthing the decisions made by management or the authority in the house, the way things are handled, directives that have been issued for the overall good of the business, family and goal. Misery loves company. The whole time you, your friends, coworkers, or family members spend murmuring and complaining, you are accomplishing nothing positive. Murmuring and complaining causes division. **Amos 3:3** *Can two walk together, except they be agreed?* Ever notice that after someone murmurs and complains, you have to stop, correct and redirect the atmosphere and thinking before you can go on to get things done? Success does not live where murmuring and complaining reside and operate.

We are in fact commanded NOT TO MURMUR again in **Philippians 2:14** *Do all things WITHOUT murmurings and disputings.* Dictionary.com defines ²murmuring as: complaining in a low tone or indistinctly. Whining and making excuses are also a form of murmuring and complaining.

Murmuring and complaining—let's see what it costs. Numbers 16:49 *Now they that died in the plague were fourteen thousand and seven hundred, beside them that died about the matter of Korah.* Remember that Korah and his clique (250 followers) started their group with murmuring and complaining against Moses. Finding fault with the way things were done and putting down the directives issued—that is certainly not the way they would have handled it. Their murmuring and complaining turned into outright rebellion against the men God had sent to bring them into their destiny. **Numbers 16:26** *And he spake unto the congregation, saying, Depart, I pray you, from the tents of these wicked men, and touch nothing of theirs, lest ye be consumed in all their sins.* **Numbers 16:30-34** *But if the Lord make a new thing, and the earth open her mouth, and swallow them up, with all that appertain unto them, and they go down quick into the pit; then ye shall understand that these men have provoked the Lord. 31) And it came to pass, as he had made an end of speaking all these words, that the ground clave asunder that was under them: 32) And the earth opened her mouth, and* *swallowed them up, and their houses, and all the men that appertained unto Korah, and all their goods. 33) They, and all that appertained to them, went down ALIVE into the pit, and the earth closed upon them: and they perished from among the congregation. 34) And all Israel that were round about them fled at the cry of them: for they said, Lest the earth swallow us up also.*

Murmuring and complaining caused plagues and death to come on the children of Israel in the Bible. Murmuring and complaining kindled the wrath of God against the Israelites. You must remember that Israel was God's chosen, called and highly favored nation of people. **Numbers 32:14** *And the Lord's anger was kindled against Israel, and He made them wander in the wilderness forty (40) years, until all the generation, that had done evil in the sight of the Lord, was consumed.*

Here, it is also pointed out to us what murmuring and complaining against God, against our man and woman of God, even against one another costs those that do it. The results are plagues, the wrath of God, and death.

Murmuring and complaining is detestable to God. He won't have anything to do with it, and deals with it quickly by "ridding" himself of it. There is no progress, increase, wealth or success where murmuring and complaining are allowed to continue to operate. Murmuring and complaining bring down morale and cause negative thinking and bad attitudes. When this type thinking goes unchecked, (a little leaven contaminates the whole lump—loaf), productivity is minimized, discouragement and downtime (even accidents on the job, due to loss of focus and full concentration on the job being done) start to happen. People begin finding reasons to miss work and not wanting to come to work at all. Murmuring and complaining is a thief that attaches itself to the hearer, much like a garbage truck dumping garbage by the truckload into your hearing, and if not cast down, they bring you down and get you off into thinking, doing and behaving in a negative way (non-productive, failure mode).

1Corinthians 10:5 *Casting down imaginations, and every high thing that exalteth itself against the knowledge (word) of God, and bringing into captivity every thought to the obedience of Christ.*

Proverbs 18:21 *Death and life are in the power of the tongue: and they that love it shall eat the fruit thereof.*

Murmuring and complaining are spirits sent to rob people and businesses of their productivity, momentum, increase, wealth, potential, progress, and sense of direction. Murmuring and complaining will hinder or stop completely the hearer, the household, and the business where it is allowed to continue from reaching its destiny (goal). Those that spend their time and energy murmuring and complaining will not live in the level of success and accomplishment God placed in each of us to attain.

Dictionary.com defines [3]complaining – to express dissatisfaction, pain, grief, censure, resentment; 2) find fault. Anytime we take our time, energy and spoken words to complain, express dissatisfaction, resentment or find fault, we place ourselves in a position to incur the wrath of God, and will not receive His blessing in that endeavor. We should certainly not ever blame God for something bad that happens to us or someone else. If you will look closely, it is the result of a wrong decision, mistake, or wrong association that made the experience go BAD. **James 1:13** *Let* *no man say when he is tempted, I am tempted of God: for God cannot be tempted with evil, neither He tempteth any man.*

Proverbs 22:10 *Cast out the scorner, and contention shall go out; yea, strife and reproach shall cease.*

Think for a moment of an instance recently when you or someone near you murmured and complained about something or someone. Write down the instance and ask God to forgive you. If it was someone else that you saw and heard murmuring or complaining, ask God to open their eyes and show them how wrong it is, (convict them in their hearts), so they will ask God's forgiveness and not do it again.

_____

_____

If it was you, ask God to help you recognize the next time you are about to engage in murmuring and complaining—since now you are aware of how dangerous it is to you and detestable it is to God.

_____

_____

Instead of murmuring and complaining, we are to take the situation to God in prayer and ask Him to make it right. As we pray, God shows us what to do and how to go about it.

Write down what God is showing you and speaking to you to do about the situation.

_____

_____

Has there ever been an instance where you blamed God for something?

_____

_____

1Peter 5:7 *Casting all your care upon Him; for He careth for you.*

Our cares, anxieties, and issues are to be transferred to God. Certainly we must take them to Him in prayer and ask Him to show us how to deal with them and how to bring closure to hurtful or wronged experiences. He longs to be invited into every detail of our lives, and that our lives would be lived in peace and abundance.

If you have an unresolved situation that comes to mind at this time, list it here.

_____

_____

Pray this prayer. Jesus, please forgive me for blaming you for this thing that went wrong in my life. I now know that you love me and want only the best, as well as only success for me in every area of my life. Help me to forgive anyone that I have been holding a grudge against because they wronged me. I know that you will avenge me and heal me of this hurt. As I release this person, I am released from the limitation that comes from not forgiving those that wrong me in Jesus' name.

Thank you, Jesus, for setting me free from this situation and the pain that went with it.

Now, list any additional experiences or situations that come to mind at this time (even the little things). Once you write them down, take the paper and burn it or shred it. This is your vow to leave it with God and go on with your life. It's gone, and it's not going to hound, harass you, or hold you back ever again.

_____

_____

_____

_____

Chapter 6

Not Spending Time & Money Wisely

Dictionary.com defines [4]waste: 1) to consume, spend or employ uselessly or without adequate return; use to no avail or profit; squander: *to waste money* 2) to fail or neglect to use: *to waste an opportunity, wasted potential, wasted talents* 3) to destroy or consume gradually: *erosion wastes shorelines*.

Mismanagement or unwise spending is waste. Waste is as destructive and harmful as procrastination. It eats away at your business and individual success. It sucks the life out of what could have been your breakthrough, the accomplishment you've worked so hard for, the goal you were only 1 step away from reaching. It stops or holds you back from obtaining your prize, your success, your increase, your wealth, your potential, the best you could have had—but now you have to live a limited version of life and business (something God never intended for you to go through). It makes a project, goal, accomplishment or dream take much longer than it should have taken.

Think about taking the long way to get somewhere, when it could have taken only a day. Remember the Israelite trip that only physically took 3 days to get there, and ended up taking 40 years. What a waste, what a mess, what a bad use of their time.

<u>Psalms 90:12</u> *So teach us to number our days, that we may apply our hearts unto wisdom.*

Here, God instructs us to consume time, spend time, employ time, and put time to work for us <u>with adequate return (productive, progressive RESULTS)</u>. He instructs us not to neglect or misuse time. Time and money are put in our hands every day—that when spent (used) properly, help our lives be successful and comfortable. We are equipped with time and money to: reach our destiny, accomplish our goals, and help others reach their destiny and goals (bless others). When we spend our time and money wisely, we live in the promises of God.

Time and money are resources placed in our hands. Time and money are resources made available to us for our use. They are to be used wisely on a daily (even moment-to-moment) basis. When we misuse or waste time and money, is it any different than wasting water and electricity? Think about it. Water and electricity are utilities that are accessed by metered use. It is measured for us, and if wasted we must pay more for it. If time and money are wasted, it is like water poured onto the ground—it's gone. Think about it. You can make more money, but yesterday at 3pm on Thursday, July, 20__ is gone. <u>You can't bring it back</u>.

Another word for spend is invest. Dictionary.com defines [5]<u>invest</u>:

1. to put (money) to use, by purchase or expenditure, in something offering potential profitable returns, as interest, income, or appreciation in value. 2. to use (money), as in accumulating something: such as education, money-making ideas and inventions. **3.** to use, give, or devote (time, talent, etc.), as for a purpose or to achieve something: such as special projects, research and development, cures for certain diseases, or advertising to reach untapped markets.

Why do we spend our time and money on things that will not accomplish the things we need to get done? Why do we spend our time and money on things that will not cause us to have what we need? Why do we spend our time and money on things that will not cause us to attain the quality of life and things we need to live comfortably, to educate ourselves and our children on what God has to say about the matter (needs, situations, problems) we face daily in our lives. Why do we spend our time and money on things and social circles that will not assist us in reaching our goals, making our dreams happen, bring out the best in us, and cause us to fulfill our destiny?

Take a few minutes to think about:
What have you been spending your time and/or money on that will not accomplish the things you need to get done?

_____

_____

What have you been spending your time and/or money on that will not cause you to get what you and your family need? List them below.

_____

_____

What have you been spending your time and/or money on that has nothing to do with attaining (reaching) the quality of life and getting the things you and your family need to live comfortably?

_____

_____

Have you invested any time and/or money in finding out what God has to say about the needs, situations, or problems you are facing daily in your life? This should be in the form of focusing on scriptures on the specific need, situation, or problem and prayer.

_____

_____

What have you been spending your time and/or money on; such as material things and social circles that will not assist you in reaching your goals, not assist you in making your dreams happen, not bring out the best in you, and not cause you to fulfill your destiny?

_____

_____

IF you have LACK, check yourself for SLACK !
Use what you have!
Proverbs 18:9 *He also that is slothful (lazy, inactive, slack) in his work is brother to him that is a great waster (destroyer).* You don't have time to be wasting time. Spend your time and money wisely, or become a SLAVE to both! Dictionary.com defines [6]<u>destroy</u>: to reduce an object to a useless form; to demolish, ruin, put an end to.

Time is money. If you don't use (spend) your time and money wisely, you waste them.

Waste is time and money spent unnecessarily on things that are not needed. Then, when you do need something, the funds are not available. Some decisions you make can be so damaging financially and time consuming that they may take years to correct. <u>The decisions you make, the way you spend your time and money, affect all who are connected to you</u>. Think about it. <u>The way you spend your time and money affects your business, your job, your life as an individual, your spouse, your children, your destiny, your quality of life—and theirs</u>.

Keep your priorities straight.
Keep balance in your life.
Watch and <u>pray about everything</u>.

<u>You Get Results When You</u>:
1. Use what you've got.
2. ARE Obedient to the Word.
3. Expect God to come through for you!

When we don't spend our time wisely, we never have enough time to get the things done that we need to do. Then we begin to feel overwhelmed, mentally fatigued, frustrated, pressured and easily agitated. When our children, our spouses, or our bosses ask us to do just one more thing, we feel hassled. We need to spend our time wisely, so we make the most of every day. We need to spend our time wisely so we remain balanced. When we don't spend our time wisely, we become a slave to time. Time seems to crowd us. Time seems to be our enemy—instead of a resource that we command, utilize and get the most out of (utilize to its fullest potential). We need to make the most (get the most done) in every 24-hour period that we can. Otherwise; procrastination (putting off till another day, another time what you can do right now), excuses and underachievement become a way of life. Just one more time of not doing what you know you should have gotten done today, becomes one more day of "putting off until later." Soon you become undependable to your family, your friends and your employer. Dependability is a key to being all God intended you to be.

Proverbs 25:19 *Confidence in an unfaithful man (undependable person) in time of trouble is like a broken tooth, and a foot out of joint.*

You become the person no one wants to be around and can't take anything they say seriously because they can't be depended upon for anything. Your children only know your empty promises, because you no longer come through on anything you say you will do with them or for them. All of us know someone like that—and we do our best to steer clear of them (or put ourselves in a position to not ever need them for any reason).

Another example is the person who only does what they absolutely have to—there is no excellence in them. Promotion never comes to the person who does only what they absolutely have to, because the employer (and their family) know they can't be depended on in a crunch or crisis to do whatever it takes to get the job done.

Proverbs 20:13 *Love not sleep, lest thou come to poverty; open thine eyes, and thou shalt be satisfied with bread.*

Proverbs 24:33 *Yet a little sleep, a little slumber, a little folding of the hands to rest: 34) So shall thy poverty come as one that travelleth; and thy want as an armed man.*

Proverbs 21:25 *The desire of the slothful killeth him: for his hands refuse to labour.*

The world calls this Enemy to Success, Mismanagement. Both time and money become taskmasters (you enslave yourself to them when you don't manage them wisely).

Observe the people around you who mismanaged their money and mismanaged their time. When you don't spend time and money wisely, you seem to never have enough of either. Life becomes miserable—sometimes even seems not worth living. Keeping your priorities straight is a big part of spending your time wisely. Keeping within your budget is a major part of spending your money wisely.

Good Stewards over time and money. If we don't spend them wisely, they become our enemies. If God cannot trust you with the money you currently have (the wages you currently earn), why would he increase you and give you more? It would only cause your problems to multiply.

Matthew 25:23 (NIV) *"His master replied, 'Well done, good and faithful servant! You have been faithful with a few things; I will put you in charge of many things. Come and share your master's happiness!"*

If you waste time, you waste opportunities to earn money. Once you earn the money, you don't spend it wisely, so you never have enough money to take care of what needs to be paid. You always feel short on money, because you didn't spend it when and where it was supposed to be spent. The first thing you do when you get paid is to set aside 10% for tithe.

Matthew 6:33 *But seek ye first the kingdom of God, and His righteousness; and all these things shall be added unto you. (You will have everything that you need.)*

Malachi 3:10 *Bring ye ALL the tithe into the storehouse (God's house) then all else will be added unto you.*

90% of all arguments/fights in marriages are about money (finances). You feel strapped when you don't have money. Your time, energy and thoughts constantly gravitate to money and how you are going to earn (get) it—then, what you are going to do (spend) it on as soon as you get it. You borrow (advances) on your paycheck.

Did you notice how God's law is 10% tithe, He promises to bless (increase, multiply, cause to succeed) the other 90%. HOWEVER, if you don't give Him the 1st 10% off the top (off your gross income); He doesn't bless the other 90%. Notice that the above statistic "90% of all arguments/fights in marriages are about money (finances)". Exactly 90% is the amount God promises to bless abundantly—beyond your wildest imagination, beyond your biggest need. And 90% is the number of arguments and fights that result when that 10% is not met. NO COINCIDENCE. Now watch the corresponding results in the paragraph below.

You charge up your credit cards—instead of using them for emergency only. Emergency use of credit cards is where you pay the amount charged in 30 days—or you don't use the card. That way, you never overcharge on your credit card, and you don't rack up amounts on your credit card that will take years to pay off. It's easy to get sucked into that type spending, charging, buying way more than you KNOW you will be able to pay off in the next 30 days. You are only digging a financial pit for yourself when you continue that kind of spending.

Proverbs 22:7 *The rich ruleth over the poor, and the borrower (person charging—person overspending) is servant to the lender.*

How can you position yourself for success, for wealth, for increase, to obtain your goals, and reach your destiny, if you are in credit card debt over your head? You are even worse off than the Israelites coming out of Egypt. When the Israelites came out of Egypt, they were loaded!

This should get you angry!!!

At least the Israelites came out of their slavery (bondage) to Egypt and Pharaoh. <u>But your lack of discipline with your time AND your money has become YOUR PHARAOH</u>. You did it to yourself. You can't blame anyone else.

Try this simple exercise: Think about the places you have gone in the last week, and the last month, that you spent more than you should have. List them here. Place a dollar amount on the money you spent there. List it at the end of Line 2.

_____

_____

_____

Think about the things you've purchased in the last week, and the last month that you really didn't need. List them here. Place a dollar value on the total amount you spent on things you really could have done without buying. List it at the end of Line 4.

_____

_____

Higher Levels of Success

See how quickly these 2 areas add up over only 30 days time…now if you were to list and track these same 2 areas of spending for 12 months, what would the total be?

Do you ever consider how much you overspend just because you don't compare pricing before spending? Spending more than you have to for a product or a service is overspending. When you discipline yourself to only spend what you have to (comparative shopping), then you always enjoy savings, and always get the most out of the money you earn. When you overspend, you are throwing your money away.

Think about this. Just because a merchant advertises a SALE, doesn't mean there is savings involved for you if you shop there. But you won't know that unless you do comparative pricing BEFORE buying from that store. Sometimes merchants advertise a SALE to get the buying public into the store, and markup the item before starting the sale. Again, no savings involved for you, the consumer. But, how would you know that if you have not done your price comparisons for the items you are in the store to buy.

It's easy, quick and is most inexpensively done online. Just browse the store "weekly ads" on the internet. There are coupons available while browsing online that help you save hundreds of dollars on the items you were going to buy anyway. Instead of driving to several stores, decide on 1 that has the greatest amount of items you were going to buy anyway—on sale. Try to buy several (if your budget allows) when you see that item on sale. Then you will not have to pay regular price for that item. The same items go on sale again approximately every 6 weeks.

Chapter 7

Arrogance or Haughtiness

Proverbs 16:18 *Pride goeth before destruction, and an haughty spirit before a fall.*

Proverbs 6:16-19 *These six things doth the Lord hate; yea, seven are an abomination unto Him: 17) A proud look, a lying tongue, and hands that shed innocent blood, 18) An heart that deviseth wicked imaginations, feet that be swift in running to mischief, 19) A false witness that speaketh lies, and he that soweth discord among brethren.*

Ezekiel 30:6 *Thus saith the Lord; They also that uphold Egypt shall fall; and the pride of her power shall come down: from the tower of Syene shall they fall in it by the sword, saith the Lord God.*

Obadiah 1:3 *The pride of thine heart hath deceived thee, thou that dwellest in the clefts of the rock, whose habitation is high; that saith in his heart, Who shall bring me down to the ground?*

Zephaniah 2:10-11 & 3:1-2 *This shall they have for their pride, because they have reproached and magnified themselves against the people of the Lord of hosts. 11) The Lord will be terrible unto them: for He will famish (reduce to nothing) all the gods of the earth; and men shall worship Him, every one from this place, even all the isles of the heathen. 3:1) Woe to her that is filthy and polluted, to the oppressing city! 2) She obeyed not the voice; she received not correction; she trusted not in the Lord; she drew not near to her God.*

Proverbs 21:24 *Proud and haughty scorner is his name, who dealeth in proud wrath (acts in arrogant pride).*

Once you begin to accomplish goals, reach some levels of success, and attain wealth, you should never look down on anyone. You should never think you are better or more than another person or another company. God hates this. You should always remember where you came from. You should always give and try to help those less fortunate than you. You should always "give back to the community". The community can be the place where you lived when you grew up, or some person, group or charity that helped you along the way. It can be some person, group or charity that God pointed out to you as you were diligently working to attain your success, your goal, the level of wealth, increase, and knowledge that you have now. God wants us to share the knowledge and understanding we obtain with others who do not yet understand—so they can come up in their understanding and their knowledge and have a better quality of life. None of us rolled out of bed one morning "knowing it all". If we walk around, looking down on others (a haughty look), thinking that we have it all and know it all, that is when we have set ourselves up to be toppled down off our high pedestals (that we placed ourselves on). When people applaud us or compliment us on a job well done, or how much we have accomplished, or how well we have done, we need to not get puffed up. Knowledge has a way of "puffing" up those with degrees, so they think they don't need God. We must guard ourselves from ever going there. It is a dangerous place to be. Even if we do it for only a short time, we endanger ourselves from being "taken down a couple notches".

Proverbs16:18 *Pride goeth before destruction, and an haughty spirit before a fall.*

When you see this scripture, be certain that God is swift to carry out the destruction and fall of pride and haughtiness, because even Lucifer (Satan, the devil) acted in pride when he thought himself to be equal to God and took 1/3 of the angels in heaven with him. Pride <u>DANGEROUSLY DECEIVES</u> those that allow it to camp out in their minds and hearts. Haughtiness is that way of looking down on others and thinking in your heart and mind that you are more than them, because....1) of what you have; 2) who you are; 3) what level you have attained spiritually, physically, financially, emotionally, college degree (PHD); 4) even your geographic location—thinking that calamity would never strike that place. God has a way of reaching us all—wherever we are. He is the only one that can give us <u>TRUE PROTECTION</u>. If you think <u>ANY OTHER WAY, YOU ARE DECEIVED</u>.

Businesses and individuals fall all the time because they get into this thinking. Then they begin acting a certain way that shuns and looks down on the very people they should be selling to, servicing, helping, serving, and assisting. It can be the small business man/woman just getting started that needs to know what to do and what pitfalls to avoid during the first five (5) years of operation. It can be that new-hire that just joined your staff and needs to fit in and get started on the "right foot". It can be that college graduate that has so much book knowledge and a degree to put to work, but doesn't have a clue what's required in the work force—yet. (It takes both book knowledge AND on-the-job experience to succeed in life.) It can be the new kid in class or new neighbor in the neighborhood that needs to see a smile of acceptance or hear a "Hello, I'm _____. If you need any help finding things around here until you get settled in and familiar with where everything is, just ask."

You see someone less fortunate than yourself, and you make fun of them. Sometimes people make bad choices that put them in that situation, but some just never had anyone to give them a better example, and accepted what "Life handed them". They never had anyone teach them that you don't have to be a product of your environment. You don't have to accept the negative reports and negative words that society and men's reports/assessments try to label you with. Look at all the people walking around, and talking perfectly well that doctors said would never walk and talk again. Look at all those who overcame obstacles and weaknesses to accomplish their goals, projects, and dreams.

"Except by the grace of God, There Go I", a famous statement and cliché made by John Bradford, an English Reformer and martyr. That person, in that situation, could have been you—but by the grace of God ONLY, were you spared from being in that wreck, born in that family, grew up in that neighborhood, surrounded by losers, not ever wanting more in life, not ever being encouraged—always being told, "you'll never amount to anything, you'll never be nothing, you're so dumb, you don't know nothing", or "be real—look at who you are, you don't stand a chance". Someone, somewhere, at some time or another, encouraged each one of us to do better, be better, have better, think positively, go farther, want more, not settle for less than God's best in any and every area of our life.

James 1:14 *But EVERY man is tempted, when he is drawn away of his own lust (desires), and enticed (seduced—talked into doing something you wouldn't ordinarily do).*

After reading this chapter, were there any instances that came to mind where you thought you were more than another person? Jot them here, then ask God to forgive you. Ask Him also to point out to you instantly if you ever even begin to do it again.

_____

_____

Have you ever looked down on someone's misfortune and thought "How could they let that happen?

_____

_____

When was the last time you looked down on another person—whether it was due to their way of life, the way they dressed, the place where they lived, or their situation?

_____

_____

Have you ever said something to another person without first thinking how it might possibly make them feel small, insignificant, or put down?

_____

_____

If you have honestly answered "Yes" to any, or all of the above questions, you need to repent and ask God for His forgiveness. Otherwise, you open the door for "destruction and a fall" to come upon you. The world today teaches this type of thinking and behavior. **Proverbs 6:16-19** *These six things doth the Lord hate; yea, seven are an abomination to Him: 17) A proud look, a lying tongue, and hands that shed innocent blood, 18) An heart that deviseth wicked imaginations, feet that be swift in running to mischief, 19) A false witness that speaketh lies, and he that soweth discord among the brethren.*

Chapter 8

Lack of Planning

Luke 14:28 *For which of you, intending to build a tower, sitteth not down first, and counteth the cost, whether he have sufficient to finish it?*

Habbakuk 2:2 *And the Lord answered me, and said, Write the vision, and make it plain upon tables, that he may run that readeth it.* Write down your dream. Investors, banks and other lending institutions require a 3-year, 5-year, even a 10-year plan from businesses before they agree to lend them ANY money. This is to make CERTAIN the borrower, the business owner has given much thought and strategy in the planning stages of business startup. We, too, must plan in order to attain our goals, dreams and reach our destiny. We have to continue working toward the goal, the dream—or else become distracted, discouraged, stop before we reach our destination (our destiny). You've heard the saying, "Keep your eyes on the prize". What is your prize? You can have several. You should have one financially, physically, spiritually, family-based, and personally. Is one of your prizes career-wise or academic prize?

Are you WILLING to pay the cost? It may mean you have to turn off the television, get off the telephone, spend time praying, reading the Bible, studying books that have been written to edify (buildup) the believer in the things of Christ to come closer to God, and to be able to HEAR from God what the plan is, what the next step needs to be, what the solution is, what is the right job for you, which house is the right house, right career, right vehicle, right location for that business, right mate, right business partner, right decision, right path forward to get the project completed by that seemingly impossible deadline, right people to get the job done, right employee to hire for that position.

How much thought, planning, considering-what-it-will-take to get there have you done? What will it take to make that happen in your business, in your family, in your life? Have you spoken to people in that type of business, or in that career? Have you spoken to people that you see around you that are already experiencing that level of success or that very goal you have set for yourself? Talk to them to find out what was involved from startup to completion. Find out what pitfalls to avoid, what to stay away from, what worked for them, and what they tried that didn't work for them. Even before you approach them by phone or in person, have a list of questions ready with paper to write down notes of the information they tell you. Gathering information and planning is THE MOST IMPORTANT step in moving forward and getting started, towards reaching your goal and accomplishing your dream.

My Co-Pastor, Sherry Potters, once told me, "Preparation time is NEVER wasted". These are <u>Words of Wisdom</u>. Sometimes, we might be tempted to minimize, cut short, or completely cut out the time we should be spending in preparation for whatever phase we are in, while working toward our prize, project, goal or dream. Don't cut out the details along the way. "An ounce of prevention is worth a pound of cure" "Hindsight IS 20/20". These quips and quotes come from people who again and again experienced failure. They foolishly gave up the level of <u>success they could have had</u> and the level of success God always intended for them, because they became impatient and thought they could cut short what was TOTALLY NECESSARY to reach their prize, project, goal or dream. Ask a painter what happens if you cheat or cut out a step in "prep time". <u>You end up with a mess and have to START ALL OVER AGAIN</u>. Ask a painter what happens if you do all the necessary steps, then get impatient and not allow the paint to completely dry after all that hard work and time you spent preparing the area to be painted. <u>You end up with a mess, and have to START ALL OVER AGAIN</u>. Every day, every project, every goal, every dream is like a canvas. We start with a fresh, empty canvas, and as we 1) Seek God first, dedicating our prize, project, goal, and dream to Him, asking Him what it will take to make it happen. 2) Talk to others that have accomplished that task, project, prize, goal, and dream 3) Write the plan down, listing what it will take to get the prize, project, goal, and dream completed and make it happen—so we don't overlook or miss an important NECESSARY DETAIL that is needed to make it happen successfully, 4) work out every detail it takes to make it happen.

    You have to see yourself attaining that prize. Olympic gold-medalists do this exercise at least once, if not daily while training—before they win.

Plan the work, then work the plan. Any prize, project, goal, and dream worth having, is worth the work it is going to take to make it happen.

In that same vein, God is telling us to consider, think really hard about, be serious, and accept what it will take to complete the project, reach the goal, accomplish the career, make the dream happen. Sometimes, once we really find out <u>all that is involved</u> and <u>all that is required</u>, we realize that we don't want to have to do all that, or cannot realistically commit to doing all that is required to make that thing happen.

Better to gather information and make an informed decision, than to find out (realize) halfway or ¾ the way, that this is way more than you should have taken on. We also need to take into consideration what our life will be like after the purchase or the decision is made. What does the maintenance of that car involve? What does the maintenance of that appliance involve? Does that house or townhouse or apartment have an HOA (Homeowner's Association) that enforces certain restrictions that will cost you money or you will have to hire someone make that happen and stay in compliance with the rules and requirements?

Make sure you ask questions and get all this factored into your decision before you "sign on the dotted line". Any time there is a signed contract involved, you need to ask all the questions you can about what is involved BEFORE you sign, instead of jumping in with all the hype the salesperson is giving you about how good you look, and how grand life is going to be, and everything will be so fine; only to find out afterward what is involved and required of those who live there. Sometimes, I've found that the savings they were offering was to make up for requirements or downsides that the tenants and new owners were going to have to live with. Do your research. Ask the questions. If you don't know what questions to ask, take a parent or mentor with you—that's not childish, that's wisdom. They know what to ask before you sign, so you don't get stuck in a binding contract, or a payment plan that ends up costing you 3-4 times what you borrowed (what the appliance, car, or house purchase price was). What seems like the best thing that ever happened to you, can turn out to be your worst nightmare if you don't ask the right questions before signing or purchasing.

Ask anyone who ever got caught in an "upside down" situation after having purchased a car, home, or townhouse. They ended up owing more than the vehicle or house was valued (worth) and were stuck paying the difference. If they did sell it, they had to pay the difference BEFORE they could purchase another one for themselves to live in or drive. For example, GAP insurance is one of the best decisions you can include in your purchase when you buy a car. It <u>will pay</u> any money owed on the vehicle if it is totaled during an accident and you are "upside down" in your note. It will keep you from owing thousands of dollars on some vehicle you can't even drive anymore. What a nightmare…

Major decisions in life (especially) require proper planning. Planning can be as simple as gathering information so you can make an informed decision. What do I mean? Major decisions include: marriage, purchase of house, car, career, career change, college or technical college (are you better with your hands, or book savvy). Just in the decision on whether or not to go into it. Just in the decision on whether to take on that additional project, goal, and place your child in that extracurricular activity that will stretch you even thinner than you already are. We don't like to think about this, but major decisions are also made after the death of a loved one, or an accident that renders family members disabled.

What project or major decision are you facing right now?

_____

_____

Have you asked God to show you what to do and how to go about it? Ask Him to give you guidance, direction and instruction to successfully accomplish the project and make right decisions in every phase thru to completion.

_____

_____

Have you talked to someone whom you can trust that has already successfully accomplished that project or faced a similar decision to gather information of all what is involved, and what things/situations to look out for (pitfalls to avoid); deadlines or requirements to be aware of, and what costs that are included?

_____

_____

Now that you have gathered the information and possibly gotten some estimates from 3 recommended sources, (always take best out of 3), you are ready to move forward and make it happen.

Think about any major decisions you are going to be making in the next 6-12 months. NOW is a good time to begin gathering information and doing research (internet), phone calls (let your fingers do the walking), and talking to successful people whom you know have been through a similar purchase or experience and came through it without drama, heartache, hardship, or bankruptcy.

Forward thinking is a new term used to get us to anticipate the need and "count the cost" in all areas and aspects of our personal lives and in business. It affects our thinking, our behavior, our decision-making, our actions, our decisions not to react, and the way we look at things throughout each day. It affects whether we have success or failure, and it affects the level of accomplishment/success each day will enjoy... or endure. You decide.

What projects, goals, accomplishments, places you want to travel to have you thought of, but they still seem so far away. You have probably said to yourself, "I'll get there someday". Or maybe you said, "I don't have the money to go there". Every trip worth taking, and place worth traveling to is worthy of planning when you want to go, how you plan to get there, what places you want to see once you get there, and how much money it will cost to completely cover the costs of the trip. Then you can make your reservations ahead of time. You can start putting aside the money you will need to make your vacation (planned stay to the place you've always wanted to go see and experience) happen. Even schedule your time off from work early in January (instead of the month before). Plan one here.

Chapter 9

Instability

James 1:8 *A double-minded man is unstable in ALL his ways.*

James 1:13 *Let no man say when he is tempted, I am tempted of God: for God cannot be tempted with evil, neither He tempteth any man.*

Definition: [7]double-minded – wavering or undecided in mind.

Definition: [8]instability - tendency to behave in an unpredictable, changeable, or erratic manner: *emotional instability.*

We need to remain constantly and consistently the same in our standards and our walk with God in order to progress to and fulfill our destiny. Men and women who are unstable in their attendance and diligence at work, or their contributions to their family responsibilities and relationships don't have relationships that work or last very long. Work relationships consist of 2 parties that each produce (sell) something that will benefit the other.

Both parties must agree that they will give at least 100 percent to the relationship in order to make the relationship succeed. Whether in business or personal relationships, both parties must agree on what percentage they expect to receive from the relationship and what percentage they expect to give. If the relationship is unbalanced (i.e. 60/40 or 80/20) the giving party quickly becomes frustrated, feeling "used" and "taken advantage of". Both parties must always work toward a 50/50 percentage of giving and receiving, or the relationship will not work.

When you are unstable and inconsistent spiritually, mentally, emotionally, financially or physically, you cannot make any progress. Those around you—your family, your friends, your employer, your business partner(s) cannot depend on you to anticipate the need or act in their best interest—because they don't know when you will stop thinking straight. They don't know when your behavior will give way to wacky, erratic decisions that aren't in the best interest of the family, or of the work needing to get done on the job, in the marriage (or other serious) relationship, or in the best interest of your children. Think about it. All around you every day, people depend on you to think clearly, rationally, positively, lawfully, and kindly. When we don't, people get hurt—sometimes they get killed. It could be in traffic. It could be on the job. It could be after you get home. It could be on the school or college campus. It could be in your neighborhood.

Instability can stem from imbalance in your life. If you don't have a healthy balance of work and rest time, you create an imbalance. If you don't have a relationship with God, family, co-workers, church members, friends outside your workplace, home and church (acquaintances). We all know that we must maintain healthy balance in our lives spiritually, mentally, emotionally, physically and financially. Any time any of these areas experience an imbalance, we are going to have trouble in our lives. That is without any outside pressure, external unplanned circumstances beyond our control or uninvited interference. So now it is easy to see that imbalance leads to instability. It is the first step. It just goes downhill from there if not addressed and corrected. We must not "blame" or use imbalance as an excuse. We must identify the imbalance (possibly a priority that's out of order), and <u>correct it QUICKLY</u>. The longer a priority or imbalance is allowed to remain out of order, the greater the consequence (damage) it will cost you. Oh yes, it will cost you. It will cost you time, money, and some level of heartache and/or hardship. If you've never thought about it that way before, ask those who have dealt with a family member on drugs, alcohol, gambling or depression.

Unforgiveness is a type of imbalance. Oh yes it is. When you have unforgiveness in your life, things will not succeed (or the level of success will be marginal in comparison to what it will be once you forgive and release whoever wronged or hurt you). **Matthew 6:12; Matthew 14-15** *12) And forgive us our debts (sins), as we forgive our debtors (those who have hurt and wronged us). 14) For if ye forgive men their trespasses, your heavenly Father will also forgive you: 15) But if ye forgive not men their trespasses, neither will your Father forgive your trespasses.* So, unforgiveness clearly limits ANY success and to what level of success you will experience in your life—and how long your success will last.

Philippians 3:13 (NIV) *Brothers, I do not consider myself yet to have taken hold (attained or arrived) of it. But one thing I do: Forgetting what is behind (insisting that you will not live in the past) and straining toward (insisting on moving toward) what is ahead, (the project, the goal, the career, the degree, the dream, the vision, overcoming limitations) 14) I press on toward the goal to win the prize for which God has called me heavenward in Christ Jesus.*

How can you possibly move forward, make progress, overcome obstacles and limitations and succeed if you are constantly gravitating BACK to old thoughts, old behaviors, old experiences, and old ways of doing things? YOU CAN'T. It is insanity to think that you are going to get ahead or succeed by doing the same things you did in the past when your life was so messed up or your business was going downhill. You determine to take control of the matter, the situation, the business situation and turn it around for your good. God does it for us every day...if we just invite Him in (through prayer) to turn every situation around for our good. Instability lives where people can't seem to "GET PAST THEIR PAST". GET OVER IT !

That is certainly a limitation in itself. Living in the past; constantly thinking about the past; bogging down in the moment, the situation, the turmoil, and the effects of the wrong decision STOP YOUR PROGRESS. It also causes instability, because it causes imbalance and minimizes clarity in the way you see things, in the way you think, and the way you respond to situations, respond to people, and the decisions you make. Unstable.

God wants us to see that holding on to the past is one of the root causes of instability, so we can correct it, and

MOVE FORWARD. We have to make a decision, and a determined (on purpose) effort to daily GET PAST OUR PAST—whether it is a business deal gone bad, or a relationship that did not work (probably was not meant to be and was not good for you). Even though we determine to get past the business deal or business relationship or personal relationship gone bad (just ended), the drama, the process of separating and getting started again or going on with your life and your children without that other person is a process that takes time. Think about divorce. Think about the death of a business partner, parent, spouse or other loved one. During the process of getting life, business and job back on track, we have to constantly and on-purpose fight off (when necessary and plow through—deal with) those memories, those feelings, those images and experiences that tend to replay in our minds over and over and over again EACH DAY. We have to ask God to help us GET PAST OUR PAST, so we don't become unstable and bogged down in it. That is where depression, discouragement, mental fatigue and exhaustion like to set up camp— if we let them.

Can you think of area(s) in your life where you seem to be "Bogging Down". It's just hard to get over that. It just seems to keep coming back in your mind, and stopping you from getting on with your life. Take a moment to list them below.

Spiritually: _____

Mentally: _____

Emotionally: _____

Physically: _____

Financially: _____

Have you ever observed someone driving a car? At some point, for whatever reason, (perhaps the driver lost focus for a moment—maybe a split second), and one of the wheels went off the road. The wheel hit a pothole or loose gravel. The driver has to carefully, but quickly adjust the steering to get all 4 wheels back on track, so the car can resume the trip and arrive safely at its destination. Perhaps it was raining, and the driver unaware drove through a patch of water, and the wheel never even left the road, the driver never even had to lose focus. The wheel just lost traction. At that moment an imbalance (instability) came into the picture. Sometimes the driver can correct the imbalance in time. Sometimes the driver overcorrects, and then loses control of the vehicle. The vehicle goes into a spin—sometimes hitting and damaging other vehicles. Sometimes it hits or crashes into telephone posts, lampposts, concrete culverts, embankments or buildings. Sometimes the driver lives to tell about it. The driver learns from their imbalance, identifies what caused it, and knows how to avoid it from happening again. Sometimes they don't live to figure it out.

Think for a moment of those (5) areas of your life. Can you pinpoint any imbalances? Jot them down.

Spiritually: _____

Mentally: _____

Emotionally: _____

Physically: _____

Financially: _____

Think about how major or minor the imbalances are. Remember that small repairs (imbalances) are easier to solve and correct than those left unresolved, uncorrected, unaddressed. Take care and be a good steward of those people, those responsibilities, and those assignments (tasks, projects, goals) that have been placed in your care and to you.

Also be aware of responsibilities and other people's problems/issues you might be taking on that are not for you to handle. Let those around you handle their own problems, and remember you can't fix everybody's everything. Only God can do that.

What will it take to correct that imbalance and bring balance back into that area of your life?

Spiritually: _____

Mentally: _____

Emotionally: _____

Physically: _____

Financially: _____

If it is not clear or obvious to you what it will take to correct the imbalance and what the most direct and precise answer is, ask God to show you what to do and how to go about it. Ask Him to give you wisdom and revelation in all these areas, so that you will continue to keep all areas of your life in balance and keep stability in your life at all times.

3 John 1:2 *Beloved, I wish above ALL things that thou mayest prosper (succeed) and be in (good) health (every bit made whole), even as thy soul (mind, will, emotions, reasoning and intellect) prospereth.*

Chapter 10

Greed

Dictionary.com defines [9]greed - 1) excessive desire, as for wealth or power, fame, praise, knowledge; 2) excessive consumption of or desire for food; gluttony.

The Bible refers to greed as "covetousness". **Luke 12:15** *And He said unto them, Take heed, and beware of covetousness (greed-excessive desire): for a man's life consisteth not in the abundance of the things (material things) he possesseth.*

Mark 7:22-23 *Thefts, covetousness (greed - excessive desire), wickedness, deceit, lasciviousness, an evil eye, blasphemy, pride, foolishness: 23) All these evil things come from within, and defile (contaminate, pollute) a man.*

Proverbs 1:19 *So are the ways of every one that is greedy of gain; which taketh away the life of the owners thereof.*

When people give into greedy behavior, they forget that God is watching what they are doing, and how they are going about it. They start "stepping on" whomever they need to, just to get what they want. Greed is fueled by selfishness and lasciviousness (lack of self-control). In reality, greed is lust. Lust for money, wealth, power, material things, beauty, glamour, fame, or food. Greed is never satisfied. Greed consumes the person acting in greed, and drives him or her to get more. Greed is a demonic spirit that causes the person to manipulate and take advantage of others to get what they want at any cost. Greed causes people to kill others, steal, cheat and lie to get what they want. **James 4:2-3** *Ye lust, and have not: ye kill, and desire (covet) to have, and cannot obtain: ye fight and war, yet ye have not, because ye ask not. 3) Ye ask, and receive not, because ye ask amiss, that ye may consume it upon your lusts.*

Ephesians 5:5 *For this ye know, that NO whoremonger, nor unclean person, nor covetous (greedy, obsessed, maniac) man, who is an idolater, hath any inheritance in the kingdom of Christ and of God.*

Luke 12:15 *And He said unto them, "Take heed, and beware of covetousness (greed): for a man's life consisteth not in the abundance of the things which he possesseth.* Greed is never satisfied. Greed is obsessed with gathering and obtaining wealth—and never has enough money or material possessions. Greed always wants more. Greed wants what others have, and will lie, cheat, steal and sometimes kill to get it. Greed justifies whatever it does and sees nothing wrong with what it does to get what it wants.

Greed loves money and material things more than God.

Can you think of anything you have ever loved more than God?

___

Can you think of anything you ever put before God—instead of putting God first?

___

Can you think of any situation you have been in where a greedy person used you to get what they wanted?

___

Can you think of any situation you have been in where you used someone (took advantage of a person) to get what you wanted—even though, deep down inside you knew it was wrong?

___

Can you think of any situation where you ever tried to control and/or manipulate someone else to get what you wanted?

___

James 1:14 *But EVERY man is tempted, when he is drawn away of his own lust (greed, excessive desires), and enticed.*

Dictionary.com defines [10]<u>enticed</u>: to lead on by exciting hope or desire.

1 John 2:15 *For all that is in the world, the lust of the flesh, and the lust of the eyes, and the pride of life, is not of the Father, but is of the world.*

<u>God will not be mocked</u>. Whatever was gotten (attained or accomplished) through greed or wrong motives, will not be blessed, multiplied, or caused to succeed by God. God only blesses those things that glorify His name.

Galatians 6:7 *Be not deceived; God is not mocked: for whatsoever a man soweth, that shall he also reap.*

James 3:16 *For where you have envy and selfish ambition, there you find disorder and every evil practice.*

Greedy people do not succeed in business. Greedy people do not succeed in life. Greedy people lose what they have gotten through greed. Greedy people don't get to enjoy the benefits of the wealth and material goods their greed attained for them.

Part Two
Positioning Yourself For Success

Chapter 11

Position For Transition (Increase)

1. <u>Get Your Mindset Right</u>

In order to grow and increase your company, succeed in your project or assignment, and move forward in your life, you must first get your mindset right. You must begin to think "expansion", "increase", and "no longer small". You must re-train your thought processes to think MEGA. Mega-minded thinks exponential (unlimited potential)!

2. <u>Get Your Past Experiences Out of Your Mind</u>

What you did in the past that did not work, as well as any bad experiences you may have had—anytime you continuously think about how this didn't work for you in the past or that didn't work for you in the past, you limit yourself. Anytime you allow flashbacks of bad experiences to come through your mind and dwell on them, you limit yourself. Anytime you allow things that have been hard or unattainable for you in the past to deter you from trying them again, you limit yourself. (Just remember, you still need to count the cost—consider everything that will be involved in completing that project.)

3. *Accept Your New Season*

You must embrace your "New Season". You must make sure to live in the "NOW" and not in the past. Whatever habits, schedules, possibly even friends you had in your "Old Season" or your past (the situation, plateau, old relationship, old job, old church) you just came out of, must be put aside. That was then, this is now. What worked then, won't work in your new season! What worked in that old relationship, how you did things at your previous job, how you interacted, or even the places you went together with that old friend or church group should no longer be how you do things. It's a new day, a new season, and a new level. The way you think, the way you look at things, the way you respond to situations and people in your life (your behavior), the way you dress, your lifestyle, the way you work—smarter, not harder, the way you operate (plan and attain) your daily, weekly and monthly goals needs to be adjusted and adapted to your new season. You MUST no longer operate in a small-minded way, but with MEGA-minded intentions, plans and goals. Even the way you talk—make it a point to speak only positive things, and things that line up with the word of God. We must make it a point to spend time only with Godly counsel. **Psalms 1:1-3** *Blessed is the man that walketh not in the counsel of the ungodly, nor standeth in the way of sinners, nor sitteth in the seat of the scornful. 2) But his delight is in the law of the Lord; and in his law doth he meditate day and night. 3) And he shall be like a tree planted by the rivers of water, that bringeth forth his fruit (RESULTS) in his season; his* *leaf also shall not wither; and WHATSOEVER HE DOETH SHALL PROSPER (increase, enlarge, multiply, succeed).*

Spend time only in Godly (divine) relationships, appointments and connections. **Psalms 1:4-6** *The ungodly are not so: but are like the chaff which the wind driveth away. 5) Therefore the ungodly shall not stand in the judgment, nor sinners in the congregation of the righteous. 6) For the Lord knoweth the way of the righteous: but the way of the ungodly shall perish.*

4. Dress For Success

Successful people remain attractive at all times! You MUST dress for success. Even if you are just going to the mailbox or to the grocery store, you must dress attractively (not necessarily in a 3-piece suit). Your hair should be groomed attractively and women should have their makeup on—no curlers, sweatsuits, or flip-flops. You never know whom you will meet on the way, or once you get there!

5. Continually Anticipate & Expect God

Successful people re-train their minds, wills, and emotions to continually anticipate and expect God to move in a dramatic way that will bless, enlarge, increase them as individuals, increase their influence, increase their abilities, and increase their effectiveness in each and every situation in their lives, each and every day. If your anticipation and expectation is not active and functioning every day in every situation, you are not allowing God to have free reign and movement in every aspect and detail of your life. Remember, He increases (enlarges the territory), multiplies (increases the growth and potential), prospers, and causes EVERYTHING He is involved in to succeed!!!

6. *Prepare for the Part!*

Small-minded thinking causes you to do only what is absolutely necessary to get things done. For instance, instead of allowing yourself only 20 minutes to get ready for an appointment or workday, you allow yourself an hour. Decide which outfit you will wear and hang it outside your closet the night before the important event. If it is your first time traveling there, map out your route the night before. Instead of allowing only 30 minutes to get to your destination or job, leave a little early and don't rush. Leave yourself enough time for unexpected bottlenecks in traffic or other delays. MEGA-minded people plan ahead. They constantly think about ALL the things that will be involved (required) to: attain, make that bigger idea, larger facility, increased production, promotion on the job, increased effectiveness in their work and on their jobs, increased influence in their workplaces, in their relationships (Work, Family, Church, Social—Friends), in their neighborhoods, communities, as well as their network of acquaintances.

7. *Preparation Time is NEVER WASTED*

You are constantly drawing all types of business to you right now! You have untapped markets to access and explore. You have untapped resources to research and connect with to begin utilizing what has been available to you all along—you just didn't know about it. You have untapped networking abilities and contacts (people who are connected with the companies, markets, skills and products necessary to enhance what your business has to offer).

While you were reading the chapter on "Position for Transition (Increase), what areas needing your attention and/or adjustment came to mind so you can properly be positioned for transition?

_____

_____

Were there any areas of "Accepting Your New Season" that need more planning? List them here.

_____

_____

Now, think about what will be involved to make that expansion happen. What additional requirements need to be met on your part to attain the increase in the area that came to mind? List it here.

_____

_____

Because preparation time is never wasted, ask God to show you if there is any additional preparation that needs to be made, so that you can truly be positioned to receive your increase and expansion (enlarged territory) from Him. List the steps of preparation He shows or instructs you with here.

_____

_____

Chapter 12

Get Ready For The Transfer Of Wealth

You must position yourself for the transfer. You must 1) pray, 2) spend your time and money wisely, 3) remove the clutter from your life, 4) seek God for divine guidance, direction and instruction on every decision and at the beginning of every day, and 5) remember to give thanks and praise daily for the accomplishments of that day/week. Begin to see yourself in the place you want to be. Whether it is a better job with better pay, a larger home, a better car or a marriage made in heaven (that you are enjoying right now here on earth)—a marriage made for dominion.

Luke 16:10 (NIV) *"Whoever can be trusted with very little can also be trusted with much, and whoever is dishonest with very little will also be dishonest with much.*

God has to be able to trust you with more, before He will give it to you. How well are you taking care of the apartment or home you presently have? How well are you taking care of the truck or auto you already have? How responsible are you with taking care of all the details necessary to do your job thoroughly, completely, and with precision? Do you go out of your way to make sure your boss/supervisor doesn't have to "tell you everything"? Why would anyone promote a micro-managed mindset that has to be reminded of what they should be doing next?

If you cannot be trusted with a small business, a small situation, a small group of people, a small sector of industry, how can God make you a ruler over much? You need to master the situation, the problem, overcome the limitation, master the level of success and responsibility, the level of accountability, and level of stewardship at the level (place) where you are now. Then, God will give you more. Once He sees He can trust you with what He has already given you stewardship over, THEN he will trust you and award you the bigger business, more employees, more of the market, more money to use, a larger home, a luxury vehicle. Why would you expect God to give you more if you can't even be trusted to manage, spend properly, and take care of what you have right now?

Promotion comes to the employee who comes forth with solutions—not problems. Promotion comes to the employee who doesn't mind digging in and getting the job done in a pinch—even though it may not be in his/her "job description". Promotion comes to the employee who anticipates the need of the employer—or mentions to the supervisor/employer when they see something coming up (cause/effect) that would require additional supplies/manpower/security be put into place before the fact, instead of after the fact. Promotion comes to the employee who is there consistently—and if they must miss work, they try to minimize the impact of their time away from that position. Promotion/raise comes to those who have shown God that they can be trusted to be good stewards of the money/income they already have coming in.

Promotions and increase are to be understood and looked upon as a "level up". The world sees promotions on the job, and increases in volumes of sales and business as "luck", "charisma", or something the world owes you. None of these are true. Promotions and increase are from the Lord and the Lord alone.

Deuteronomy 8:17-18 *And thou say in thine heart, My power and the might of mine hand hath gotten me this wealth. 18) But thou shalt remember the Lord thy God: for it is He that giveth thee power to get wealth, that He may establish His covenant which He sware unto thy fathers, as it is this day.*

Psalms 75:6-7 *For promotion cometh neither from the east, nor from the west, nor from the south. 7) But God is the judge: He putteth down one, and setteth up another.*

As you were reading the chapter on "Get Ready for the transfer of Wealth", what areas came to mind that need to be adjusted (prayer, time seeking God, removing clutter, completing unfinished matters, maintenance habits (or lack of them)? List them here. What day and time is a good time to make these a constant in your schedule? List them here.

Chapter 13

We Have Everything We Need To Fulfill Our Destiny!

Everything you need to fulfill your destiny was placed inside you before you were born. How can that be? It is already inside us and all we have to do is develop it and start using it in our everyday lives to get to where we are going.

Our destiny begins to unfold—like a story in front of us. We can do more than we used to. Those things that used to challenge us are no longer a challenge, but a minor adjustment in our day. Those things that used to be impossible or a struggle are not such a big deal anymore. You begin to wonder what was so hard about it, and why it gave you a hard time.

Every day, God provides (supplies) what we will need for that day. IF this has not ever occurred to you, you need to meditate on it—and utilize each item (resource) He has placed at your disposal to its fullest potential.

Much like your mother, caretaker or older sibling used to lay out your clothes every morning for you to wear that day, God lays out (places at our disposal) what we will need for that day. He places resources within our reach. You've heard of the phrase "tapping into our resources". Our resources are 1) people 2) finances, 3) witty ideas, 4) fresh angles (approaches, markets, strategies, answers to our prayers) to accomplish what you need to get done in your work, your life, your needs being met.

1. *People Resources*
God causes individuals to come into our lives on a daily basis to network with to help us accomplish what we need to do. When we do this, we utilize or use the resources God gives us. It might be a person or persons we work with every day, an acquaintance, or someone He might have come into our lives and help us just for this one day, this one time. Thank them and treat them well, but DON'T FEEL OBLIGATED to this person, God sent them for this need — on this day. **2 Chronicles 16:9** *For the eyes of the Lord run to and fro throughout the whole earth, to shew Himself strong in the behalf of them whose heart is perfect toward him.*

2. *Financial Resources*
Sometimes it comes in the form of a check in the mail; sometimes you receive bonuses, commissions, referral fees, rebates, loan reimbursements, refunds, bargains or discounts. Your financial resources are monetary blessings that God puts you in contact with so you can make the transfer come to pass.

3. *Witty Ideas*
Witty ideas come from God. We ask Him to show us and download to us the witty ideas that can come only from Him. He has unique and fresh ideas that come

from "thoughts that are higher than our thoughts and ways that are higher than our ways". **Isaiah 55:8-9** *For my thoughts are not your thoughts, neither are your ways my ways, saith the Lord. 9) For as the heavens are higher than the earth, so are my ways higher than your ways, and my thoughts than your thoughts.* However, if we ask Him daily to download witty ideas to us, He will gladly download them to us and we can use them to attain greater effectiveness, greater influence, and greater impact, accomplish our goals and achieve greater levels of success on a daily basis.

4. Fresh Angles

Philippians 3:15 *Let us therefore, as many as be perfect (mature), be thus minded: and if in any thing ye be otherwise minded, God shall reveal even this unto you.* Changes don't usually come instantly—either in business or in our personal lives. But when the things we have been doing aren't producing results (aren't working), we are to continue to be stable, consistent and constant in walking out the things we know are right and necessary to carry on production in our businesses and our homes. We are to persist during economically unstable times. We are to persist when the news looms negative projections of doom and financial recession. When the business industry changes overnight in our businesses, or something unexpected (crisis or other type situation) in our family lives—we need to persist with prayer, a positive attitude, and a fresh angle.

He allows us to see things as He sees them and understand them as He understands them. When you observe things from a higher elevation (imagine for a moment God's panoramic view of everything as it takes place on earth). When you ask God to help you see things as He sees them and understand things as He understands them, and deal with every situation and opportunity as He deals with it or handles it, you get a "Higher Level" take on the matter. His angle and His elevated insight into the root of the problem and the solution immediately remove you from the "bottom feeder" or "ground level" observation deck and bring you to new levels to see, understand, deal with, overcome, and overtake— progress and success.

For instance, when you are in a job search or approaching a new, previously untapped market, you need to remain well-read and informed. This will assist you in keeping a positive attitude while you persist. As you read the latest, cutting-edge articles on product and technology updates, you gain knowledge and information. This keeps you "in-the-loop" and abreast of what is the latest in technology, which is an ever-changing market. We need to stay informed of what type market is prevailing in our specific business. What is in demand? As you do this, you keep a healthy, informed, positive attitude and remain a productive part of what's going on—instead of getting into thought processes of "what's passed you up" or "being passed up" thinking. Industry calls it "Forward Thinking". This same principle applies to job searches as it does to new market acquisition.

5. *Answers To Our Prayers*

We know that we are in God's perfect will when our prayers receive results (we see the answers to our prayers right before our very eyes. **1 John 5:14-15** *And this is the confidence that we have in Him, that, if we ask any*

thing according to His will, He heareth us: 15) And if we know that He hear us, whatsoever we ask, we know that we have the petitions that we desired (asked) of Him. We must pray through to the breakthrough. There is a prayer of insistence that people pray, expecting and insisting that they <u>will not be denied</u>. **Genesis 32:26** *And he said, Let me go, for the day breaketh. And he said, I will not let thee go, except thou bless me.*
What is it that you've asked God to help you with, but have not yet received your answer to? List it below. We must continue to pray, believe, and thank Him for the answer to our prayer. At that point, we have placed it in His most capable hands and entrusted it to the <u>only</u> One that can make it happen. <u>It shall come to pass</u>.

_____

_____

6. <u>Our Needs Being Met</u>
God is the need-meeter. **Philippians 4:19** *But my God shall supply all your need according to His riches in glory by Christ Jesus.* God is in the business of meeting our needs. Just the same way we make sure our children have what they need to get their school work done (reports, homework, projects, tutoring), to be their best when playing on a sports team (right fitting and right type equipment, uniform, knowledge of the game, practice to be the best they can possibly be), God makes sure we have everything we need every single day. Employers make sure their employees have the proper on-the-job training, safety equipment, and breaks to get the job done successfully and safely. Needs are

constantly being met. We are to look to God, our provider (spiritually, mentally, emotionally, physically and financially every day). You're Going to Need This!

While reading the section on "Our Needs Being Met", were there any needs that came to mind? List them here.

Spiritually: _____

Mentally: _____

Emotionally: _____

Physically: _____

Financially: _____

Now, pray and ask God to meet that specific need (or needs) the way He promised He would in Philippians 4:19 above, in Jesus' name.

Chapter 14

You Have The Anointing

Y ou have it IN YOU—the enablement, ability, capacity, and the power to succeed. The enablement, ability, capability and power to do what before you could not do, because now God is with you. **Isaiah 41:10** *Fear thou not; for I am with thee: be ye not dismayed; for I am thy God: I will strengthen thee; yea, I will help thee; yea, I will uphold thee with the right hand of my righteousness.*

Psalms 1:2-3 *But his delight is in the law of the Lord (the Word of God); and in his law doth he meditate day and night 3) And he shall be like a tree planted by the rivers of water, that bringeth forth his fruit in his season; his leaf also shall not wither; and WHATSOEVER HE DOETH SHALL PROSPER (succeed).*

Jeremiah 29:11 *For I know the thoughts (PLANS) that I think (have) toward you, saith the Lord, thoughts (plans) of peace (success), and not of evil (failure), to give YOU an expected end.*

Where there is vision, there is provision. Everything God touches succeeds. Everything God is involved in succeeds. Everything God tells you to do, He blesses. So, as you allow God to guide, direct and instruct you on a daily basis, your business, your influence, your effectiveness, and your accomplishments will grow, increase, multiply, prosper and succeed.

Joshua 1:8 *This book of the law shall not depart out of thy mouth; but thou shalt meditate therein day and night, that thou mayest observe to do according to all that is written therein: for then thou shalt make thy way prosperous, and then thou shalt have good success.*

As you were reading this chapter, certainly God showed you some of the abilities, enablements, and capabilities He has placed in you. List them here.

_____

_____

Prayer of Thanksgiving: Thank you, Lord God, for ALL the enablements (anointing), gifts (talents), abilities and capabilities you have placed within me. Now I ask you to stir them into operation. Show me where to put them to work in my life in Jesus' name.

Prayer of Preparation: Holy Spirit show me clearly the enablements, gifts, abilities or capabilities that need to be trained and developed before they can be put into use, please direct me to the church or development program that will assist me in getting trained and developed in that enablement, gift, ability or capability in Jesus' name.

Chapter 15

Use The Resources God Has Given You!

Proverbs 3:5 *Trust in the Lord with ALL thine heart; and lean not unto thine own understanding 6) In ALL thy ways acknowledge (seek and inquire of) Him, and He shall direct (show you how to go about it) thy paths.* **You have the Wisdom of God to know how to use the Resources He Has Given YOU !**

Every day, God places at our disposal (just like our mother or caretaker laid our clothes out for us to get dressed every morning). God lays out the resources and provisions we will need to get the assignments and work done that He wants us to get done or completed for that day. It is our responsibility to access and utilize every resource, every provision, every divine connection and contact He places at our disposal (puts us in contact with) to get the work done that day. If we do not, we are wasting time, resources, and displacing ourselves from being fit (available and accessible) for the Master's Use.

Our daily prayer should be, "Help me (cause me) Lord to access and utilize every resource, connection (contact) and provision that you have placed (made available) for me to do the work you intended for me to do while I am here on this earth. Help me to be ALL you intended me to be and do ALL you intended me to do EVERY DAY in Jesus' name. Ministering angels have been placed at our disposal to assist us in: 1) being ALL God intended us to be; 2) accomplish ALL God put us on this earth to accomplish; 3) help one another; and 4) access and utilize to its fullest potential ALL the resources and divine connections God placed within our ability to access and utilize.

Hebrews 1:14 *Are they not all ministering spirits, sent forth to minister (help and assist) for them who shall be heirs of salvation (born again believers)?*

Think about the resources that God has made accessible to you. If you haven't really thought about this before, God was showing you while you read this section. What resources did he point out to you that are available to you? Jot them down.

_____

_____

Now think about this. Have you sincerely been putting the resources God has given you to the full use and potential He gave them to you to use?

_____

_____

Ask God to help you see and utilize all the resources He has given you and placed in your hands to succeed in every area of your life. Then make a note of how you will begin to use them more wisely and be a better steward of the resources He has given you. Thank Him for all He has done, all He has given you, and the wisdom to make right choices in Jesus' name.

_____

_____

_____

_____

Chapter 16

Focused Commitment To The Vision

Keep your <u>eyes on the prize</u>. **Philippians 3:13** *Brethren, I count not myself to have apprehended: but this one thing I do, forgetting those things which are behind, and reaching forth unto those things which are before, 14) I press toward the mark for the prize of the high calling (upward movement) of God in Christ Jesus.* Due diligence—that's doing what it takes to make the dream become a reality. Doing what it takes to complete the project. Doing what it takes to reach the goal. Sometimes we don't realize what is involved when we make up our minds we are going to do something. But, we have to finish.

Effectiveness is a MUST!

We must be effective in every area of our life and in every situation in our life in order to have TRUE success. Effective with people, effective with skill and communication, effective with co-workers and customers. Effective with our family members and neighbors. Effective in our work and on our jobs. Effective and stable.

Gaining And Maintaining Momentum

In order to be successful, you have to streamline your methods of working, so that you work as efficiently as possible to gain momentum (get the most work done in the time that you have to do it). By doing this, you meet your deadlines without feeling exhausted and worn out. Keep to a schedule where you tackle your biggest projects or harder tasks when your energy is at its highest. Do not attempt to begin a large project towards the end of the day. Try to reserve time toward the last 15-30 minutes of every day planning what you will do, and what order you will do it in when you arrive the next day. Remember not to get off-task, or distracted by others who are not committed to accomplishing the same things you are. Not everyone wants to go the distance to get the prize and realize their dreams. Not everyone is willing to make what is important to you, important to them. Your priorities will probably not be the same as others. Some don't even have priorities.

Adapting And Changing To Grow And Enlarge

Your thinking must enlarge to accommodate the growth that comes with success. You must remain open-minded to different ways of doing things—getting the results you need in a new, more streamlined, cost-effective way.

Always Gaining New Ground

You are moving forward. The first step to attaining your new level, accomplishment, success in life is to see yourself in that setting, home, job, career, size of clothing, lifestyle, economic status, married, single, with children, empty-nested, on vacation, new location, after the promotion...

Effectiveness and Influence (or Lack of It)

Effectiveness in every area of our lives, WE MUST HAVE IT. Our effectiveness is determined by our prayer life, our passion for our assignment or goal, our determination, our faithfulness (loyalty) to the cause, our endurance, our knowledge about all factors pertaining to that area (situation, location), and our resourcefulness.

Lack of Effectiveness, in short is lack of results in our lives.

Influence with those around us. SUCCESSFUL PEOPLE HAVE IT. The level of influence is determined by our prayer life, our lifestyle, our behavior (our witness), and our attitudes. Influence is determined by our knowledge of what is truly effective with those around us. The ability to influence those whom you do business with, work with, live with, worship with should not be confused with "manipulation and control" which is witchcraft and a Jezebel spirit, but a gift and a skill which MUST be developed and continuously sharpened. God knows our hearts. The intent of the heart is what makes your influence blessed and ordered by God or simply manipulation and an abomination to God. Think about it. People will cooperate with you, go out of their way to help you, go above and beyond the call of duty—and the letter of the law to help you when you have influence. They will take extraordinary measures to see that you do not fail—and get the necessary results; get more than you even asked for, <u>when you have influence</u>.

Matthew 5:13 *You are the salt of the earth. But if the salt loses its saltiness, how can it be made salty again? It is no longer good for anything, except to be thrown out and trampled by men.*

When you read this scripture, read it again and insert "influence" in the place of "salt". Now I know that God has told us not to add one jot or tittle to the word of God. He also showed me that when "influence or light", "revelation", "knowledge", "understanding" "flavor", "set apart for the Master's Use" is inserted when this scripture is read—illumination and revelation bursts forth! So, we see that influence is an element that is vital and essential to success in every area of our lives. Think of people that have influenced your life. A parent, a teacher, a spiritual leader or pastor, a friend, a business partner or loved one. They not only helped you through difficult, challenging, trying situations that were anywhere from trivial to life-altering on the scale of situations (things we have been through) in our lives. Some of them we prayed for, others required intercession into our lives by people that God assigned to pray for us at different intervals and situations in our lives, some were divinely intervened into our lives as God moved on our behalf, and spared and guided us away from destruction and utter ruin.

While you were reading the section on Effectiveness, what areas in your life did God bring to mind that needed greater effectiveness? List them here.

_____

_____

_____

_____

If we are being truly honest, we will recognize that <u>every</u> area of our lives and businesses need greater effectiveness—every day! As you pray today, ask God for greater effectiveness in every area of your life, every aspect of your business, and every aspect of your academics (for children in school and young adults in college). You are operating in some level of effectiveness now—or else you wouldn't be reading this book! What most of us don't understand or think forward enough to pray, is that the level of effectiveness that got us through yesterday and enabled us to complete our last assignment or project won't get us through today.

The level of effectiveness that worked for you in your previous level of success was good for that level. Now you need "greater effectiveness". Effectiveness is good for the day, the job, project, goal, assignment, and level of success you are in right now. Once you get through that, you need greater for the next level. So, you pray daily for greater effectiveness. There's an "aha moment".

Once you begin praying this way, you should come back to this section and list how the different aspects and areas of your life have changed with improvement. You should see and list the levels of accomplishment and success that have increased because you incorporated that prayer into your daily prayer requests. <u>More Results</u>. List them here.

_____

_____

_____

_____

<u>John 15:2</u> *Every branch in Me that beareth not fruit (does not show results in its life) He taketh away: and every branch that beareth fruit, he purgeth (cleanses) it, that it may bring forth <u>more fruit</u> (more results).*

Chapter 17

New Levels Of Success Require New Levels Of Commitment

New levels of success require new levels of commitment. Whether you are working in your Business or your Personal Relationships, new levels of success require new levels of commitment. Commitment in time spent with that person, commitment in making what is important and necessary to that business important and necessary to you. In a personal relationship, a new level of making what is important to them important to you is an ongoing process and totally necessary. Times, trends, marketing strategies and demand change in the business arena. Types of commitments and levels of commitment must be made to accommodate the needs arising from enlargement and increase. When this is done, your business, your individual life, and your family will continue to progress to the next level as these changes in commitment are made.

Commitments in personal relationships, people's interests and needs change with time, age, and major events in their lives. These changes come from birth, death, marriage, divorce, graduations, job or career change (planned or through loss of previous job), major auto accidents, loss of a house, and other major financial changes. Some are the result of bad choices and decisions, but some were not at all within the control of the people involved. The commitment must remain constant and consistent. It is during these times of major change and uncertainty that businesses, employees, and personal relationships require and rely on our stability, commitment and reassurance even more to get through and over the hurdle caused by the change.

When the challenges and weights of daily business activity and personal daily life threaten our progress, our increase, our advancement and our success— adjustments must be made. In these instances we need to press on, maintain momentum, and not feel threatened or fold. Those challenges may come in the form of unexpected expense, unforeseen change in plans, change in industry standards, or demand in the marketplace.

Think about commitments that have changed in your life, in your business, and the lives of your wife (husband) and children as you have advanced to higher levels of success in different areas of your life. List them here.

_____

_____

_____

_____

As you overcome limitations, and rise to higher levels of success, you will notice how those around you are affected. Some will adjust easily to flow with the next-level of success and the changes that are necessary to flow with that increase and success. Some may question why these adjustments are necessary and resist the changes—causing a disruption of the flow. Ask God to give all of those affected the grace to flow, be flexible and embrace the adjustments so there will be no resistance during the adjustments in Jesus' name.

Chapter 18

New Levels Of Success Require New Levels Of Responsibility

Luke 12:48 *But he that knew not, and did commit things worthy of stripes, shall be beaten with few stripes. For unto whomsoever much is given, of him shall be much required: and to whom men have committed much, of him they will ask the more.*

You wanted that new car, you wanted that new house, but you must also want the added responsibility (financially, maintenance-wise, and any additional time and work—upkeep) it will require of you to keep it up and keep it going. You wanted that bigger yard—so your children would have place to run and play, but now you have to mow, weed-eat and trim the edges of that yard. All your time off work is now being consumed by the "yard work". You don't even have time to run and play with the children anymore, because you always have to be doing "yard work". You can't watch the game on television until the "yard work" is taken care of. You can't go play golf, pool or basketball with the guys until you finish the "yard work".

It seems like you have become a slave to the "yard work". Now, the Homeowner's Association is sending you letters threatening to charge you $500 to mow your yard and mulch your shrubs and trees. What have you gotten yourself into?

That new car costs more to insure because it is a newer model. The insurance premium is about the cost of another car note. When you bring that new "luxury model" car to get an oil change—an oil change costs anywhere from $89-$135. Spark plugs, which used to cost $15 to change them all, for this car costs $85 ($15-$20 each). So changing the spark plugs costs $120. Tires for this car cost about $700-800. You can't go around with economy tires on a luxury car! Wow! When I bought the car, all I could think about was how good I was going to look riding around in that car. All I could think about was how people were going to look at me differently because I was driving that car. All I could think about was "how many babes would want to be with me because I am driving that car". Now that you have that car you only have enough left (after the high-dollar maintenance is done) to go to McDonald's. The "babes" who were attracted to you realized you have "champagne taste on a kool-aid budget".

What areas of your life came to mind as you were reading the new levels of responsibility scenarios?

_____

_____

_____

_____

Hopefully, those scenarios made you laugh. At one time or another, we have all gone through at least one (if not more) situation where we decided maybe we didn't want that _____ (desired object) as much as we thought we did. Sometimes we realize (hopefully before than after) that it wasn't "all that". All that we thought it would be. It just didn't bring near the satisfaction and/or fulfillment we thought it would.

Chapter 19

Positioned, Streamlined, Ready For The Race

As we position ourselves to receive the increase, to enlarge our territory, and to accomplish ALL that God has intended for us to accomplish, attain, and do in this earth, we need to prepare. Specifically, we need to prepare to be able to manage the growth and the added responsibility that inevitably comes with increase, enlarged territory and success. We should all know that success comes with a price. The price of added responsibility, unfamiliar (sometimes uncomfortable) situations and unfamiliar events that will come up and possibly be awkward or uncomfortable at first, but when we make the necessary adjustments, we will realize that what the world calls "growing pains" is just part of the process (the price) of success, increase, and enlargement of our territory.

The adjustments will definitely come in the form of streamlining the way we spend our time and our money. Our time spent with God MUST NOT be affected by our success, increase and enlargement of our territory. We are to spend the same—if not more time praying about decisions being made, seeking the Holy Spirit's guidance, direction and instruction which is Godly wisdom for our relationships. These relationships include all the people we are associated with from business acquaintances, to business partners, to networking resources in the business world. These relationships in our social circle will need to be only those that will add value to our 1) walk with God, 2) include those who are going in our direction (only — or they will drag you down). These relationships in our family/friends/spousal circle will include spending more time with those who constantly and continuously bring you up, encourage you, and help you be all God intended you to be. Nurture and care for your wife and children; but in the friendship area, you will have to adjust the time, energy and money spent with those who take more than they give. With parents, extended family and in-laws — you must be continually aware of those that are speaking into your hearing and that those things they are speaking are in line with the word of God — or they may hinder more than promote your progress.

Adjustments will come in the form of adjusting the way we spend our time. A fresh evaluation at how we spend our 24-hours in a given day, then week will reveal what areas need to be adjusted. Write down how you are spending your time for a 7-day period, and ask the Holy Spirit to give you wisdom on how to better spend your time.

Adjustments will come in how we spend the finances we have. Make a determined effort to only spend the money you are earning, not overspending, or spending money on things that will cause you to go into debt. Try to pay off all your credit card debt and live on a cash basis (except for perhaps your mortgage). Debt-free living is how God intended for it to be. That is when we are truly at liberty to live a successful life, when we are not bound by debt on all sides. Society makes it easy to be entangled in a web of debt (credit card debt, car note debt, mortgages). Then when some unexpected expense or repair happens, it causes imbalance, crisis and sometimes putting our life-long investments at risk.

Think about it. What areas need adjustment in your life?

_____

_____

Now, what adjustments need to be made to truly make room for the increase you desire in your life?

_____

_____

Part Three

<u>Warding Off Hindrances</u>
Holding On To Your Success

Chapter 20

Take Off The Limitations...

What do you have going on in your innermost being that is causing you to be limited? Most of us don't look at "common limitations" as limitations at all. However, things you were told when you were growing up can hold you back. You take them in and push them down (repress them) and keep going like that doesn't matter. But later on when you become a young adult, then your family comes along, and inside you (the responsible parental adult), those limitations are still in there, keeping you back, holding you down. You say to yourself, "No, I've never been good at that". "No, that's not one of my strong points". "That might be easy for some people, but I could never get the hang of that."

Something someone said along the way—a parent who wasn't choosing their words wisely. That parent or person was possibly frustrated at your father or mother and said something negative to you—you took it in. A teacher who was there for the paycheck and not for the potential they saw in you—or refused to see in you. That was the element that tried to limit you—even then.

Regardless, the potential is there. Your skills have to be developed, honed, polished, sharpened, strengthened so you can be ALL YOU CAN BE, and ALL GOD INTENDED YOU TO BE. It has always been there. God sent someone along life's time frames/seasons, and path that was needed to take the time to help you develop and bring it out so you could reach your destiny. Now, YOU need to take responsibility to take your skills, your gifts, talents, goals and dreams to a higher level. There is SO MUCH MORE in store for you. So much more that God has for you if you will just link up with the divine connection that will cause you to go farther, reach higher and reach your destiny.

What the schools don't teach you is that you should find out what you are good at—what comes to you naturally (natural abilities, natural strengths, natural skills, natural interests) and go make lots of money doing it. That is what you should choose for a career. You don't need to be good at everything. People who try to do that burn out and never become as EFFECTIVE at the things God truly intended them to master, and excel at in wondrous effortless effectiveness. Ever wonder how some people do things so perfectly without even trying? They have mastered their natural God-given ability, skills, giftings and callings. They haven't tried to be good at what other people are good at. They have found their niche and are happy (totally contented) being who they are and doing what God has given them the gift(s) and abilities to do. Then they get the training and development to sharpen, strengthen, and polish those skills, choosing to make that a career using those gift(s) and skills—and make lots of money doing it.

Flowing in the natural abilities and giftings (talents) that God has placed (deposited) in you as you were being formed in the womb is what we are to do. That gives God great pleasure, and also is a form of worship to Him. He is the Creator. He has a plan for each and every one of us "predestined from when He Created heaven and earth" to do what He gave us the talent, ability, skills, and way of seeing things (each of us something different) so that when we are all doing what He gave us to do as excellently and effectively as we possibly can, The Big Picture Comes Together...What He Planned All Along From the Beginning of Time HAPPENS.

Think about any limitations that you have that must come off in order to go the next level of your success. Any limitations that are holding you back from attaining your goals, completing your projects, and making your dreams come true. Write them here.

_____

_____

_____

_____

Jeremiah 5:25 *Your iniquities have turned away these things, and your sins have withholden good things from you.*

Ask God to show you clearly what to do and how to go about overcoming each of those limitations. Write down what He shows you here.

_____

_____

Chapter 21

Get The "H" Out Of Here!!!

The 3 H's – Get them out of Your Life!

1. <u>No Hindrance</u> –

What hindrances (obstacles, roadblocks, bottle-necked and stalled plateau-situations) are stopping progress in your life? Successful people find ways around obstacles. They avoid roadblocks by anticipating the need of the projects/accomplishments they have determined to make in a given day/week/month or quarter (3-month time period). They consistently and constantly ask God to show them the answers, tell them clearly what to do AND how to go about it. Is process important? Process is TOTALLY NECESSARY. It's like a road map. We MUST strictly follow instructions—we can get there in 3 days......or 40 years. Anything in between is wasted time.

As you are reading this section, God is pointing out some things to you. What obstacles, roadblocks, bottlenecks (things standing in your way) stalled and plateau-situations are taking place in your life right now? Is it a situation with your business? Is it a situation with your job or career? Is it a situation with your marriage? Is it a situation in the life of your child? List them below.

_____

_____

_____

_____

Now ask God to show you how to overcome that obstacle and get results and accomplishments even though those obstacles are there. He is a <u>BIG God</u>, and <u>He always gets results</u>. Everything He has any part of is successful. Make note of what He is showing you to do, and how to go about it.

<u>Jeremiah 33:3</u> Call unto Me, and I will answer thee, and shew thee great and mighty things, which thou knowest not.

_____

_____

2. <u>No Hesitation</u> –

What excuses, "What if's", or procrastinations are stopping you from making a decision that must be made? What's stopping you from moving in the direction that

God has clearly signaled (instructed) you to go and what He has told you to do? List them here.

_____

_____

_____

_____

You must know that when God gives you specific instructions about a matter, He will always go with you! You are not alone.

Isaiah 43:1-2 *But now thus saith the Lord that created thee, O Jacob_____(put your name in Jacob's place), and He that formed thee, O Israel, Fear not: for I have redeemed thee, I have called thee by thy name; thou art mine. 2) When thou passest through the waters, I will be with thee; and through the rivers, they shall not overflow thee: when thou walkest through the fire, thou shalt not be burned; neither shall the flame kindle upon thee.*

Whatever trial (trouble), trying situation, uncomfortable or awkward situation or decision you are facing, God clearly states in His word printed above that He will go with you, and "He's got this". All you have to do is pray the above scripture with your name in it, believe, and He will perform it!

3. <u>No Holding Back</u> –

What passive, lackadaisical, mediocre comfort zone (rut) have you allowed yourself to settle into? This is where you do nothing or do only what you have to do to keep this one or that one "off your back" — accountability-wise.

Successful people get the "H" out of their lives.

Successful people are constantly and consistently moving forward and doing something towards where they want to be. Constantly and consistently meditating on the word of God and what God has to say about the matter (their situation).

Now that you've gotten the "H" out, make sure you are going in the right direction and pursuing (going after) the right thing for you. What is God's purpose and plan for your life? You need to know this to truly succeed and lead a fulfilled life. If you have not ever inquired of God what is God's plan and purpose for your life, ask Him now. List the answer He gives you below:

_____

_____

_____

Chapter 22

The Catastrophic "C's"

The catastrophic "C's" are so named, because they are destructive and devastating. Each one of these mindsets can become strongholds if left uncorrected. They begin subtly, but deceitfully by wandering into your mind, your business, your situations, your way of thinking (thought processes), your way of doing things (behavior), and your standards (things you accept or will not tolerate). The catastrophic "C's" will minimize your effectiveness, muffle your influence and your impact, and eventually stop your progress and success if you don't identify and stop them from operating in your business and your life.

1. Complacency– Satisfied with the way things are.

You have now reached the danger zone. You feel as though you are comfortable at the level of accomplishment you have attained. You are still riding the accolades and contentment of your latest accomplishments. Every day is a new day and a new opportunity to work things out that did not work yesterday, improve our relationship with

God and hear from Him afresh and anew. He has a fresh and new word and work for us every 24-hour period. If we are sitting back on our haunches, we will miss the next move, as well as the fresh anointing and grace needed to advance the kingdom of God, our lives, and our families for that day! We cannot afford to miss this!!!

No matter what success(es) you have achieved, you need to keep looking <u>continuously to God</u> and the future. Any other type of thinking is complacency—and a waste of precious time. **Philippians 3:12-14** *Not as though I had already attained, either were already perfect: but I follow after, if that I may apprehend that for which also I am apprehended of Christ Jesus. Brethren, I count not myself to have apprehended: but this one thing I do, forgetting those things which are behind, and reaching forth unto those things which are before, I press toward the mark for the prize of the high calling of God in Christ Jesus.*

We need to be determined to attain ALL that God meant for us to attain and accomplish when he formed us in the womb—every 24-hour period. Not only attain it, but attain it with ALL the intensity, effectiveness, impact and influence that God deposited in us, gave us the resources to attain with, and every detail completed with the thoroughness He operates in (which comes only from prayer). To be able to walk in this type of attainment and success, you have to refuse to be affected by the approval or disapproval of other people (the opinions of men).

<u>1 Corinthians 4:3-4</u> *But with me it is a very small thing that I should be judged of you, or of man's judgment: yea, I judge not mine own self. For I know nothing by myself; yet am I not hereby justified: but He that judgeth me is the Lord.*

I will go a step further and remind you that we will all stand in front of God one day and give account of what we have done and every idle (unproductive) word we allowed to come our of our mouths. At that moment, His eyes of fire will be set on YOU. Nothing else, and no one else will matter. His blazing eyes will penetrate your spirit and soul and the question will be: "Did you do what I called you to do? Were you everything I asked you to be? Did you work hard to be ALL you could for Me—every 24 Hour Period of time?" YOU will stand exposed before Him with no one to blame, and no one to compare yourself to, and no excuses to utter. It will be between YOU and Him.

Romans 14:12 *So then every one of us shall give account of himself to God.* **Matthew 12:36 (NIV)** *But I tell you that men will have to give account on the day of judgment for every careless (unproductive, negative) word they have spoken.*

Think about the 5 areas of your life listed below where you have allowed Complacency to come in and camp out (stay longer than it should—then taken root).

Spiritually: _____

Mentally: _____

Emotionally: _____

Physically: _____

Financially: _____

Pray this prayer: Lord God, forgive me for falling into the "rut" of complacency. Please show me what steps I need to take to correct any areas of complacency in my life (my job, my marriage, my business and anything affecting the lives of my children). Please alert me if complacency ever tries to creep into any area of my life ever again in Jesus' name.

List the steps of correction He shows you to take here. Now purposefully plan to put them in action today.

Spiritually: _____

Mentally: _____

Emotionally: _____

Physically: _____

Financially: _____

2. [11]**Clutter** – 1) to run in disorder; 2) a state or condition of confusion.

How can you go forward, gain momentum, or excel when your life, home, business, marriage, job, bank account—even your debt-to-earning ratio are cluttered and disorganized? We serve a God of order, structure and completion. So, plan the work and work the plan. Have boundaries set (schedules, deadlines, goals) and enforce them. Finish what you start—or don't put your hand to it!

Think about areas of your life, home, business, marriage, job, bank account, debt-to-earning ratio (credit card debt or overspending), even your mental state. Do you forget things often? Do you feel overwhelmed much of the time? Do you sometimes get home from work not remembering details of the drive home? If so, it's time to remove the "clutter" from these 5 areas of your life. When you remove the "clutter" everything functions smoothly again. If you don't, you begin making costly mistakes, overlooking things that you should have seen, and missing details that are totally necessary in every aspect of your life.

Spiritually: _____

Mentally: _____

Emotionally: _____

Physically: _____

Financially: _____

Pray this Prayer: Lord God, forgive me for allowing clutter to set up "camp" and operate in any area of my life. Please show me what steps I need to take to correct it and to avoid clutter from accumulating (in any area of my life) again, in Jesus' name.

3. [12]Confusion – 1) disorder; upheaval; tumult; chaos 2) lack of clearness or distinctness 3) a disturbed mental state; disorientation

James 3:16 *For where you have envy and selfish ambition, there you find disorder and every evil practice.*

Confusion is often a result of complacency and/or clutter. Confusion also sets in where there is envy and selfishness. Unhealthy comparisons, insecurities, manipulation (from envy and selfishness), serve to muddy the atmosphere (thereby limiting productivity, progress, and success). Confusion serves to muddy your thinking (your behavior, how you respond to situations, as well as alter the ability of your decision-making). Confusion is certain to bring about misunderstanding.

Each day, we need to think clearly (the way we think about things must be Christ-minded), see clearly (our perceptions—the way we see and filter things must be how God sees them), and respond in a positive manner in order to be productive, progress, accomplish, attain goals, and succeed. The catastrophic C's have no place where success operates.

Take a moment to jot down any of the 5 areas of your life where confusion has been trying to bring chaos and disorder into your personal life, your business, your marriage, or a situation affecting your children.

Spiritually: _____

Mentally: _____

Emotionally: _____

Physically: _____

Financially: _____

Pray this Prayer: Right now, I bind up confusion from operating in my life in Jesus' name, and I ask you Lord God, to alert me from this day forward if confusion tries to creep into any areas of my life again, in Jesus' name. Amen.

2 Corinthians 2:11 *Lest Satan should get an advantage of us: for we are not ignorant of his devices (schemes and practices).*

If you aren't moving forward, you are stagnating, complacent, becoming stale and not accomplishing anything.

Chapter 23

The Deadly "D's"

<u>**John 10:10**</u> *The thief cometh not, but (except) for to steal, and to kill, and to destroy: I am come that they might have life, and that they might have it more abundantly.*

The Deadly D's – Get them out of Your Life! The Deadly D's are 7 tools the enemy uses to get you off track, keep you from the truth and keep you from using the new angles (strategies) that will propel you into new levels of success, and keep you from reaching your destiny and your success. You must understand that if he can't stop you (your business—financially; your marriage—made for dominion and enjoyed—not endured; your children—academically and developmentally), he will do everything in his power to slow you down, keep you down, and keep you from finishing your race, living your dream, and reaching your destiny. These are the SUCCESSES in your life—or have you forgotten?

1. **Distraction**

Things that get you unfocused.

Determine that you are going to be settled, stable, and focused—no matter how much the devil tries to distract you or "dangle carrots in front of you". It is the enemy's job and primary goal to get you distracted (unfocused), cause you loss of momentum, get you slowed down, even—derailed, to the point where you are drawing back from your calling and drawing back from your assignment (your goal, your career, your dream), drawing back from your task at hand. Notice the sequence here. It's a gradual decline, but one thing usually leads to the other.

You get to college to get that degree, then one distraction (outing here, party there……they start telling you that you never do anything or have any fun) leads to the next. Soon, you are spending less and less time on your homework, your reports, and the degree that you and your parents sacrificed so diligently to make sure you received the opportunity to have. Remember why you came to college in the first place? Leave your "buzzard" friends alone—leave them behind. Your "buzzard" friends are those that are always talking about the past and how hard things are. <u>Your "buzzard" friends are not going where you are going</u>.

EVERY TIME YOU BECOME DISTRACTED, YOU DRAW BACK. When you draw back… God has NO pleasure in you. **Hebrews 10:38** *Now the just shall live by faith (trusting God to do what He said He would do): but if ANY man draw back, my soul shall have no pleasure in him.*

Connect and stay connected to your "eagle" friends. Those are the friends that make your "baby", your dream, your vision LEAP on the inside of you. Those are the people God has placed in your life that insist on remaining positive. Those are the people God has placed in your life that don't tolerate drama, mess, gossip, unproductive relationships, unproductive time wasters, unproductive conversations, money traps, etc. Notice that "eagle" friends and mentors avoid at all times, the "Catastrophic C's" and "Deadly D's", and Keep the "H" out!

It is a little more challenging on this side, but the more you stay focused and stay with it, the easier it gets. <u>Recognize this: If you know the truth and don't stand up for it, you are drawing back</u>. Do not limit the truth of God's Word to be someone's friend. Remember, not everyone is going where you are going. And, not everyone is willing to do what it takes to get where you are going.

Think about it. As you were reading the section on Distraction and Drawing Back, what areas and situations in your business, your marriage, or your children's lives did God show you where Distractions are trying to set in?

_____

_____

_____

_____

Ask God to show you what it will take to "Get Back on Track" and the best steps for you to go about it in the shortest amount of time.

_____

_____

Next time you drive by or visit a cemetery think about all the people who are represented there. Most of them died without fulfilling their dreams, without accomplishing their goals, certainly without reaching their destiny—all because they got distracted and drew back.

Why are YOU drawing back?

What areas in your business, your marriage, or your children's lives did God show you where you, your spouse, or your children have been drawing back?

_____

_____

It is necessary at this time to pray and ask God to help you 1) not to draw back again, and 2) to alert you if you ever begin to draw back in any area of your business, your life, or areas and situations affecting your children, again—in Jesus' name.

2. **Deception**

Deception is misinformation, ignorance, or believing a lie—like it was the truth. Deception not only ruins people's lives, causes misery, heartache and hardship; it kills their dreams. **John 10:10** *The thief cometh not, but (except) for to steal, and to kill, and to destroy: I am come that they might have life, and that they might have it more abundantly.* Yes, I mentioned that at the beginning of this section. But at about this point right now, it should be hitting you right between the eyes...that the enemy (the thief) wants to rob you and your children of your dreams, your strength, your creativity, your health, your ability to accomplish (reach, attain, make happen) goals and visions, your decision-making ability, your confidence in God, your future, a successful career, a comfortable and successful life. He wants to rob you of the fruits of you labor, and the rewards you have worked so hard for. So that you work and work, but are not ever able to put your hand on the compensation you so richly deserve. One of those is being able to watch your children grow up into productive, educated, accomplished, successful citizens. If he can't get to you, he will try to get to your children.

As parents, mentors, and stewards, we are to continually look out for and protect our children. They are depending on us to protect them, educate them (inform, train, develop, counsel), and keep them from harm. They have been entrusted to us from birth to (about 18 years old) when they become legally of age by law to make a living and establish a household (apartment), working to obtain food, clothing and shelter for themselves. **Proverbs 22:6** *Train up a child in the way he should go: and when he is old, he will not depart from it.* We are to raise our children, not only advising them of the things they should do to become productive, successful law-abiding citizens; but also what they should avoid (stay away from at all costs). We are to warn them of what entrapments, deceptions and predators are out there just waiting to lure, entice, take advantage of, and take over an unsuspecting, unaware, unknowing, unbelieving minded child or young adult. Even as adults, we can fall into deception—if we don't watch and pray.

When my oldest son was in 1st Grade, the teacher labeled him as ADHD and she told me he couldn't be taught. Because he would not learn the way the other 19 children in the class learned, she isolated his desk in the corner of the room where he would play at his desk most of the day. When the other children were learning phonics, of course he was not included. As a result, my son did not receive the tools he needed to read. I learned of this situation about 6 weeks before the end of that school year. I was livid. I had meetings with the principal, teacher, and the school board—who actually had sent a representative and wrote in their report that they had observed this child being isolated in the classroom. Yet, nothing had been done to make sure the child learned to read. Nothing was done to correct the teacher, correct the situation, and require the teacher to teach all the children in the class.

I vowed that my son would learn to read if I had to teach him myself. I worked with him at home. I did some research and found that there was a "transition" teacher that would take the time to get the students who needed it, the extra help they needed. I got the principal to agree to place my son in her class for the 2nd Grade's upcoming school year. I met with the teacher and pledged to stay in close contact with her 2 times each week on my son's progress. I also asked her to send home any at-home exercises we could do to help get my son's reading skills to excellence. Long story short, in the 4th Grade there was a "Read to Me Story Time" Program that my son was selected to participate in. Ironically, he was assigned and read to Ms. Wannabeateacher's 1st Grade class—the teacher who told him and me that he couldn't be taught. A "teacher" has not taught until the student has received and understood the information presented.

Matthew 26:41 *Watch and pray, that ye enter not into temptation: the spirit indeed is willing, but the flesh is weak.* Ever think or say, "That won't happen to me". DECEPTION. Ever think or say, "Just one time won't hurt you (me)". DECEPTION. Ever think or say, "No one will ever know about this". DECEPTION. Ever think or say, "No one cares about me". DECEPTION. Ever think or say, "Sticks and stones can break my bones, but words will never hurt me". DECEPTION. And the list goes on.

Deception also comes in the form of disobedience. Partial obedience is disobedience. It can be disobedience of God's word. It can be disobedience of the law. It can be disobedience of the rules at work, at school, at home. Disobedience brings loss of privileges, loss of much-needed transportation, loss of homes, loss of families and loved ones. Ask anyone who ever received a DUI or did crack. Deception is not limited to age, race, gender, socioeconomic background, demographic, educational level, or economic status. Disobedience causes loss of character and ruins integrity.

Deception also comes in the form of thinking that you know it all. An unteachable spirit or attitude is one where you won't receive instruction, godly counsel, wisdom or even protection from anyone. This is a most dangerous mindset to have. It puts you in a dangerous position. Some think they are invincible—and that it certainly won't happen to them. Our next generation is filled with this deception. I pray that God opens their eyes to the truth. **Proverbs 12:1 (KJV)** *Whoso loveth instruction loveth knowledge: but he that hateth reproof is brutish.* **Proverbs 12:1 (NIV)** *Whoever loves discipline loves knowledge, but whoever hates correction is stupid.* We should be ever learning and seeking God to show us more of what we need to know every day!

While reading this section on Deception, I'm sure God began to bring to mind specific instances and situations. What areas of your life, your business, or your children's lives that have been affected by deception came to mind? List them below:

_____

_____

You need to pray daily for God to help you to avoid deception and ensnarement of deceptive practices, and traps designed to get you, your business, and your family off the right and productive path God has for your life, your business, and your family. Deception keeps you from reaching your destiny and making your dreams happen. Only God sees the pitfalls, the deceptive practices, and the myriad (countless) forms of deception that take place every day in the world. Only by asking Him to open our eyes to them and keep us from falling into deception, ensnarement and entrapment do we remain protected and avoid them completely.

3. Disappointment

Proverbs 25:19 *Confidence in (counting on) an unfaithful man in time of trouble is like a broken tooth, and a foot out of joint.* Disappointment is the act of letting someone down, usually by promising to do something, then not doing it. Making plans and raising expectations for something to turn out well, then it turns out in an unacceptable or different way. Not having your way. Hoping that a long-awaited accomplishment or something promised will take place, and then it doesn't happen. Disappointment is one of the tools the enemy uses to destroy relationships, startup distrust, and start unforgiveness going among business partners, friends or family members.

Many shut-ins (people in hospitals, nursing homes, rehabilitation facilities and correctional facilities) have experienced disappointment when friends and family members tell them they will come to visit them, tell them they will call them and stay in touch—then don't. Most of the time, their hectic schedules and outside lives get crowded with other things. Then one day becomes a week, and a week becomes a month, and eventually 6 months or a year has passed, and the person inside the facility feels as though they've been shelved and forgotten.

Matthew 25:35-40 *For I was an hungred, and ye gave me meat: I was thirsty, and ye gave me drink: I was a stranger, and ye took me in: 36) Naked, and ye clothed me: I was sick, and ye visited me: I was in prison, and ye came unto me. 37) Then shall the righteous answer him, saying, Lord, when saw we thee an hungred, and fed thee? or thirsty, and gave thee drink? 38) When saw we thee a stranger, and took thee in? or naked, and clothed thee?*

39) Or when saw we thee sick, or in prison, and came unto thee? 40) And the King shall answer and say unto them, Verily I say unto you, Inasmuch as ye have done it unto one of the least of these my brethren, ye have done it unto me.

If we choose to make the most of a "less-than-desirable" outcome, we still win. If we choose to be flexible have a good time anyway, we still win. If we look at the upside or "bright side" and keep going, instead of getting bogged down in the flop part of what could have "ruined everything" we don't come away from that situation remembering it as a "total loss".

Think for a moment about the "Disappointments" that have taken place in your life, your business, your parents, or your children's lives. Think about a certain disappointment that made the biggest impact, or left the biggest mark in your life. What disappointment comes to mind that left the biggest mark on that situation or that person. List it here.

_____

_____

_____

_____

If that person is still here (has not gone on to be with the Lord), go to them and tell them you are sorry and want to make sure they always know you love them (if a family member) and that they are important to you. Remind them that what is important to them is important to you. (One of the sweetest things to every human being is when you make what is important to them, important to you.)

Make a commitment to stay in contact with that person on a regular basis and stay true to your commitment. It is important. Write your commitment here.

_____

_____

Ask God to forgive you for disappointing that person, and to help you do better every day, in Jesus' Name.

4. Discouragement

Proverbs 13:12 *Hope deferred maketh the heart sick, but when the desire cometh (longing fulfilled), it is a tree of life.*

Discouragement is hope deferred. Hopelessness is a dangerous place to be. Discouragement disables those who allow it to go on in their minds, wills and emotions for any length of time. Discouragement, if allowed to go down into your heart turns into depression, disablement, giving up, and thoughts of suicide. Discouragement is a major tool of the enemy. If allowed to go unchecked and not disarmed, discouragement/hopelessness turns into negativity, and a "why bother" attitude. You begin thinking this is how your life has to be. Discouragement is a major enemy to success. When you allow discouragement to stay in your mind or heart for any length of time, you will give up or "cave in". Proverbs 13:12 above warns you about this, and advises you to stay away from it. Get rid of it. It warns that the inevitable result is destruction and failure. Some people die from it! Ever hear of someone dying because they gave up the will to live? Yes, sadly, people die every day from giving up the will to live.

The enemy came to kill, steal, and destroy. Discouragement kills you by stealing your hope and your joy. Discouragement destroys your dreams, and keeps you from reaching your destiny. My parents could only take me a certain part of the way; it is up to me to take my children, and my family the rest of the way—into our promised land. They haven't come into that understanding yet. God placed me here and positioned me to be "the Link". It's up to me and God to get them there. He leads me, and as I do what He tells me to do, He will get us all there. If you allow it to, discouragement will stop you from being ALL God intended you to be, and doing ALL God placed you on this earth to do. You decide. I had to decide when my children were born that they were going to have EVERY opportunity that a 2-parent household would afford them—even though they grew up in a single-parent household. They did not choose to be born into that situation, nor did they choose to be born to the parents that bore them. They deserve the best—not the best I can give them, but the best that God promised them. So do you!

When discouragement is allowed to continue in your mind and thinking, it gives way to despair (hopelessness). Hopelessness makes people think there is no relief, no way out, and no one to help them. It places pressure on the person that's feeling hopeless to the point where the only escape they know is to end it.

Isaiah 43:1-4 (MSG Bible) *But now, God's Message, the God who made you in the first place, Jacob, the One who got you started, Israel: "Don't be afraid, I've redeemed you. I've called your name. You're mine. When you're in over your head, I'll be there with you. When you're in rough waters, you will not go down. When you're between a rock and a hard place, it won't be a dead end—Because I am God, your personal God, The Holy One of Israel, your Savior. I paid a huge price for you: all of Egypt, with rich Cush and Seba thrown in! That's how much you mean to me! That's how much I love you! I'd sell off the whole world to get you back, trade the creation just for you.*

God is the way-maker. He <u>always</u> makes a way where there seems to be no way.

What situations, experiences, decisions and/or actions of others have left you feeling discouraged or hopeless? What hope unfulfilled left you feeling like the bottom dropped out of your life? Was it a relationship or marriage that ended, when you thought it would last? Was it a business that went under because of the economy? Was it a job loss due to layoff and staff reduction? Was it a job you really wanted or a promotion you worked hard for and felt you deserved—yet it was awarded to someone else? Was it a childhood experience that left you thinking you weren't good enough, weren't smart enough, weren't pretty, weren't thin enough, weren't tall enough, weren't strong enough, or weren't rich enough? Was it the same bad experience over and over that made you feel like no matter how hard you tried you were never going to make it? List them here.

Now give them to Jesus. He has been waiting to take them and turn them around for your good. **Jeremiah 29:11** *"For I know the plans I have for you," declares the LORD, "plans to prosper you and not to harm you, plans to give you hope and a future"*.

<u>The devil has lied to you</u>. He tried to make you think there is nothing left, nothing worth hoping for, nothing left at all. <u>THAT'S A LIE</u>. God is the author and finisher of our faith (hope, courage and confidence). He created us and He has only the best for us AT ALL TIMES.

Ask God to show you the way out. Begin right now thinking about how BIG God is, and how this is a small thing for God. **Ephesians 6:10-11** *Finally, my brethren, be strong in the Lord, and in the power of His might. 11) Put on the whole armour of God, that ye may be able to <u>stand</u> against the wiles of the devil.*

In Ephesians 6:10-11 above, God tells us to stand—not cave in or give up. When we stand (on God's word), God is right there with us performing His word on our behalf. He is right there working it out for our good. He is right there turning things around to our advantage and for our benefit. He is right there making sure we have what we need. We need to stay determined to 1) stand, and 2) be strong in the Lord (determined that His word is the final authority and that God will do everything He said He would do in His word and in the power of His might).

Higher Levels of Success

Every knee has to bow in the name of Jesus. Notice He said, *"Stand against the wiles of the devil"*. Don't roll over and play dead. Don't layover like a pushover. Don't have a pity party and throw in the towel. He just commanded you to RISE UP with ALL the strength of God, ALL the stamina of God, and STAND UP TO the devil. **James 4:7** *Submit yourselves therefore to God, Resist the devil and he will flee from you.*

1 Corinthians 10:13 *There hath NO temptation (pressure) taken you but such as is common to man: but God is faithful, who will not suffer (allow) you to be tempted (pressured) above that ye are able; but will with the temptation (pressure) also make a way to escape, that ye may be able to bear (endure) it.*

You can do this. Write down what God shows you or tells you to do here.

_____

_____

<u>Anytime thoughts and emotions of discouragement or hopelessness try to come into your mind</u> to ruin your day, and to stop your momentum and progress, <u>do this instead</u>. Change the atmosphere. It is good to listen to Christian music to lighten (change) the atmosphere. Change the atmosphere with prayer. Pray for encouragement where there was discouragement before. This prayer will also change the atmosphere to remove any heaviness that may try to linger. Say this simple prayer, "I bind up discouragement, hopelessness, and any anxiety in Jesus' name". "I

loose encouragement, hope, peace, joy and strength in my mind, will, and emotions, and in every area of my life in Jesus' name".

INSIST ON: Pressing through to your breakthrough. Sometimes it seems (appears) to be "darkest before the dawn". It seems like there is no way out.

BUT, it is in that very split second, and during that very thought, that you are right on the brink (edge) of your breakthrough. Remember the woman with the issue of blood? What would have happened if she had given up? She would have ended it. She probably would have died. She certainly would not have ever received wholeness in her body. Her success was receiving wholeness (health, peace, joy and well-being). I'm sure she was able to work again and get restored to the place (financially, physically, mentally, emotionally and spiritually) that she was before that 12-year saga began. Your problem(s) have lasted 3 days, 3 weeks, or 3 months? This woman's problem lasted 12 years. Because she pressed through to her breakthrough instead of caving in, she was restored (resulted in being better off than when all that mess and everything that took place with that illness began). When you are restored, you always come out "Better Off Than You Were Before All That Happened". What area(s) and situation(s) in your life are you facing right now that you need to Press through to your Breakthrough? List them here.

_____

_____

Matthew 9:20-22: *And, behold, a woman, which was diseased with an issue of blood twelve years, came behind Him, and touched the hem of His garment: 21) For she said within herself, If I may but touch His garment, I shall be whole. 22) But Jesus turned Him about, and when he saw her, He said, Daughter, be of good comfort (take courage); thy faith hath made thee whole. And the woman was made whole from that hour.*

What made the woman whole (healed)? Her faith. Her confidence and belief that God would heal her illness and make everything all right. What is it that you haven't managed to be able to believe God for? What is it that you haven't been able to bring yourself to have confidence in Him to do for you (healing, restoration, rejuvenation, saving a loved one, forgiving you of a wrong you've committed, helping you to forgive someone who has wronged you—because you can't possibly do it by yourself? What is it that you don't believe that He will make all right? Write it here. Get it off (out of) your chest, and onto this paper.

Now, it's time to go "where the rubber meets the road". It's time to go the root. It's time to <u>make sure you have truly thought about this and not lied to yourself</u>. You can't go through life caring only about yourself and sleep at night, or look at yourself in the mirror and feel good about whom you are and what you've done. If you take lightly what God has entrusted to you. <u>It's not about you</u>! <u>Other people's lives are depending on you</u>! <u>They are depending on YOU pressing through to your breakthrough</u>. They are connected to, tied to, attached to (whether you want to admit it or not) and directly affected by YOU pressing through to your breakthrough.

<u>List here those people's names that are directly (and indirectly) affected by you pressing through to your breakthrough</u>. Your wife (or husband), your children, your grandchildren (their future, and their positioning for success) are affected. You are setting an example. Your parents, sisters and brothers — some of your relatives are affected. Your levels of business success affect your business partners, your employees (and their families). Oh yes, it does. Your breakthrough affects your co-workers, your church family, and your friends. Who else is watching you that you aren't even aware of, that needs to see you pressing through and coming through? Yes, they too, are directly affected by you pressing through to your breakthrough. Reaching their destiny is directly tied to you pressing through to your breakthrough. How far they will go, what levels of success they will attain, generations to come (out of your lineage) are affected. Whom has God entrusted to you to mentor? They are being affected. List them here.

_____

_____

_____

Are you taking you and them into their promised land, or are you quitting on the brink (edge) of breakthrough and aborting the mission? Aborting their future. Severely putting them at a disadvantage, instead of launching them to a positioning for success. ALL this is tied to your breakthrough.

That's an "aha" moment. Think about it. Write down any situations and areas of your life you have not been taking seriously (or you never saw it that way before). Areas and situations that God pointed out to you are breakthrough targets. List them here.

_____

_____

_____

_____

Breakthrough propels you to the next level. Higher levels of accomplishment, confidence, effectiveness, goals, success and destiny for your life are attained one breakthrough at a time. Each breakthrough gets you closer to your destiny. Successful people will tell you they didn't get there in a day.

5. <u>Disconnection</u>

You stopped going to church. You stopped talking to and spending time with your church friends. You stopped reading your Bible. You've just about stopped praying. Maybe every few days, you pray a little here and there—mostly when you need something or experience a little trouble. Slowly, and gradually, you are disconnecting from your power source. You are allowing an imbalance to take place in your life—<u>a spiritual imbalance</u>. When spiritual disconnection takes place, imbalance results. Expect your natural life to soon show signs of trouble, too. It is cause and effect. Everything in the natural is subject to the spiritual. When your spirit man is fed daily, your natural man will remain healthy and whole.

You NEED to hear from God daily. It is how God gets answers to you. It is how you know what to do and how to go about it. It is how God protects you and keeps you on the right track. It is how He keeps Godly counsel coming to you. It is how God spares you from deception, delays, and ensnarements. Without food, you die physically. In the same manner, without spiritual feedings (hearing the word at church, reading the word in your personal time, and hearing from God for yourself during prayer and meditation time), you die spiritually. You become separated from God. That's what spiritual death means (separation from God). When your spirit man is dead, you lose purpose. Your life becomes a series of frustrated, meaningless days of existence. You become like the world—with no answers, no joy, and lots of trouble and heartache.

Matthew 4:4 *But He answered and said, It is written, Man shall not live by bread alone, but by <u>(trusting in, relying on, obeying)</u> <u>every word</u> that proceedeth out of the mouth of God.*

Have you become disconnected from God? Just like an electrical cord cannot provide electricity to the appliance it was made to keep operating (running) when it becomes unplugged or disconnected from the power source. There is no power. There is no progress. There is no accomplishment. There is no completion. There is no success. Partial connection or "faulty connection" causes an incomplete circuit, and does not supply the needed power to get the job done.

Ask God to help you secure your connection to Him, and to help you <u>position yourself to ensure that you hear from Him every time He speaks to you</u>. One word from God is all it takes to change your situation and change your life. You will never be the same. One word takes a hopeless situation and turns it into a meaningful, amazing miracle.

List any area(s) here that came to mind as being areas that need to be secured. Faulty connections will not attain the clarity, stability, and certainty that are necessary for success.

_____

_____

6. **Darkness**

Darkness is what you have in your life when God is nowhere around. Darkness is lack of knowledge. Darkness is ignorance. Darkness is misunderstanding. Darkness is refusal to accept the truth (rebellion). Darkness is believing a lie. Darkness is disobedience. Darkness is void of light. God is light. Where there is darkness, people stumble around, run into things, have accidents and hurt themselves (injury). Where there is darkness, people are vulnerable and easily taken advantage of. Where there is darkness, there is no clarity. Where there is darkness, evil lurks and tries to snag, ensnare, and trip its prey.

Hosea 4:6 *My people are destroyed for lack of knowledge: because thou hast rejected knowledge, I will also reject thee, that thou shalt be no priest to me: seeing thou hast forgotten the law of thy God, I will also forget thy children.*

That's a staggering thought. God said in the last part of that scripture that if you forget His law (His word); He would also forget your children. Your children's success and well-being depend on your obedience to the Word. Your children's future depends on your insistence on not being in darkness and obeying the Word.

Control and Manipulation thrive in darkness.

Where there is darkness, there is no understanding. Those who are void of understanding wander around in chaos and confusion. There is no progress or success in their lives. Where there is darkness, you have all forms of vision impairment. People crash into things, continually hit their heads on a brick wall, allow strongholds to live and dictate limits and stagnation. Strongholds hold you down and hold you under, so that you continue to operate and live beneath the privileges and levels of success God intended for you, your business and your children.

Think about what area(s) and situations in your life—and the lives of your children, where you are experiencing limits, stagnation, and "keep hitting a brick wall". These are areas that are not progressing or succeeding. List them here.

_____

_____

_____

_____

Proverbs 3:5-7 *Trust in the Lord with ALL thine heart; and lean not unto thine (your) own understanding. 6) In all thy (your) ways acknowledge (pray seeking wisdom and understanding) Him, and He shall direct (make straight and smooth) thy paths. 7) Be not wise in thine (your) own eyes: (mind, thoughts, and understanding of the matter, situation), fear the Lord, and depart from evil (darkness).*

Ask God to give you clarity, understanding, and see the matter (situation) and solution to the problem clearly. What to do and how to go about it, in the name of Jesus. The answer may come in one word, or it may be as instructions. Write them here.

7. Derailment

Dictionary.com defines [13]derailment as: 1) cause to run off rails; 2) obstruct progress of; frustrate; 3) upset stability or composure of.

Derailment is distraction in its advanced stages, where it accomplishes what it came to do and that is: taking you off track. When you get off track, you don't make any progress, your stability is impeded, and frustration and delays become a part of your daily life. If you allow yourself to remain "off track" for any length of time, it will completely stop you from reaching your goal, fulfilling your dream, and reaching your destiny.

Galatians 5:7 *Ye (you) did run well; who did hinder you that ye should not obey the truth?*

You were running well, who cut in on you? Was it another influence? Who stopped you from walking in truth? Now you are living by how you feel. That is a dangerous way to live. Talk about being at-risk. Feelings are unstable—emotions will change several times in a given 24-hour period, much less in a week or a month. How can you run a business or a household based on emotions (feelings)? Up one day, down the next. Let's be real, emotions can be up at 8:00 a.m., and down by 10:00 a.m. the same morning!

Have you ever missed your exit? Derailed. God now has to redirect you. God has to take you through some minor adjustments that are unfamiliar, uncomfortable, to get you back on track, so you can move forward once again toward your destiny. As He leads you on the back roads the way will seem slower, less attractive. Be patient during this time, because God is doing what He needs to do to get you to your destiny. Obedience is the key. God is the only one who knows how to get you there!

Get back on the interstate (back on the right path, back on track), and you will get your momentum back. Ever think about how losing your momentum causes loss of progress in a major way? Wow, swerving off the path of progress. Taking the wrong exit off of the most direct route through your journey. Turning onto the wrong road to accomplishment. All those derailments cost you precious time and money. Derailments cause you to completely miss your destiny. Even if you do manage to reach your destiny, did you reach it in 3 days or 40 years? Sound familiar?

Derailment (distraction in its advanced stages) is when you become a couch potato. Television is the way your time away from work is spent and you don't ever accomplish anything at home. You don't ever accomplish anything in your personal life. You don't ever spend quality time doing things with your family because you are engrossed with the television and your level of energy and interest in anything else is gone.

Derailment (distraction in its advanced stages) is when you cease to invest time in yourself (physical fitness, reading books, doing research, having a hobby, eating healthy). You don't take care of yourself anymore. You don't care what you look like anymore. You lose interest in being your best. That expensive piece of exercise equipment you bought and used for about 3 weeks, then started using it for a clothes hanger/dryer and monument to fitness that no longer interests you—is no longer important to you. Because your physical fitness and well-being are no longer important to you...

Derailment (distraction in its advanced stages) is when you spend hours on end in front of the computer. You don't spend time with your family. You don't spend time on physical fitness. You don't ever spend time outside getting fresh air, exercise, and sunshine (necessary for a balanced, healthy lifestyle). Your computer has consumed you. One website leads to another. Your world consists of the monitor in front of you. Nothing else and no one else matters. When you get home from work, the first thing you do is turn on the computer and sit in front of it. Before you realize it, it is 12:00 midnight, and another evening has completely passed you by. Your family, friends, and children don't even know you anymore, because you have become disconnected with any social interaction. You even eat your meals at the computer—something you said you would not ever do.

Derailment (distraction in its advanced stages) is when that project you started 3-5 years ago is still sitting there, unfinished. Incomplete projects are results of derailment. Hoarding is a result of derailment.

Derailment (distraction in its advanced stages) is when you become addicted to electronic games. Being consumed by electronic gaming is a result of derailment. You (or your child) don't spend time outdoors getting fresh air and playing outdoor games anymore. You become disinterested in anything that is not part of the game. You become frustrated and even angry at those who interrupt or stop you from completing the level you are working on. You become frustrated and even angry at those who require you to limit your time on the game. You even become violent when the game is ended due to a family meal, time with the family, or outing. Your time away from work and school is spent gaming. You become disinterested in family, family functions, church, friends, pets and any other social interaction that would take time away from gaming. You become socially disconnected with everyone and everything. Your school work begins to suffer, your interest in education, academics, sports, and physical activity is no longer important.

Derailment (distraction in its advanced stages) is when you become so engrossed in that new friendship, relationship, and time spent on the phone. That cell phone is always on your ear. You can't seem to put it down. You feel the need to be constantly talking or spending time in the company of that person. You are almost co-dependent. Same with texting. You can't seem to put it down. It consumes your time, your interest, and your energy. It gets to the point that nothing else matters. You become oblivious to other people around you. You begin to ignore your surroundings, your safety and the safety of others. Your responsibilities are not important anymore. They take 2nd place, when they were supposed to be your 1st priority. You begin taking unsafe risks like texting behind the wheel of the car, texting when you should have all your attention during class, on the job, and during family dinner time.

Higher Levels of Success

While reading the section on Derailment, what area(s) or situations came up in your mind about your business, your life, your relationship with your wife, something in the lives of your children? List it here.

_____

_____

_____

_____

That situation didn't just happen overnight. Notice each time another example was cited, a specific detail was emphasized. <u>Derailment is distraction in its advanced stages</u>. That means it has been going on for some time. It needed to be corrected. You knew all along that you had responsibilities you needed to take care of, but you ignored them. You brushed it aside, like it didn't exist—it didn't matter. It needed to be kept in a healthy balance, and kept within reason. But the person falling into the trap kept putting the derailment first, instead of what was really important. Until it finally got to the point of consuming that person's time, that person's interest, and that person's energy. Once you reach that point, nothing else matters.

Not only did it cause you to lose momentum, it completely halted any progress you were making. Remember the tortoise and the hare? The friends, neighbors and co-workers that were working along side you have now passed you up, completed their projects and assignments. They have moved on to something else.

Think about it. What situations have gotten out of hand (derailed) in your life, your business, or those of your wife (husband) or your children. It's time to assess your progress (or lack of it). Jot it down.

_____

_____

What do you need to do to correct the derailment?

_____

_____

_____

When you become so consumed with the things that caused you to derail, you miss a lot of things. You tend to overlook the things that are important in running your business. You tend to overlook things that are important to your boss (and your job). You tend to overlook things that are important to your wife (your soul mate and partner), your children—who depend on you for protection and guidance as they grow up. The "flags"—warning signs, go up here and there. One today, three tomorrow—but you never saw it coming. It got to you, and now you are consumed by something that should never have received/taken that much of your time, attention and energy.

Think about it. What "flags" have been going up in your life, in your business, on your job, with your wife, in the lives of your children that need to be addressed and taken care of? These "flags" (warning signals) that are going up around you are not something you imagined. Those around you are seeing them, also. Stop and get back on track, before something terrible happens. By allowing Derailment issues to continue in your life, you position yourself for loss and destruction. You put yourself at risk: at risk of losing your business; at risk of losing your job; at risk of losing your wife; at risk of losing your children—especially, teenage children.

During their teenage years, that's when you need to stay in tune to your teen's needs, interests, and warning signs (behaviors and mood swings) even more attentively. Once you allow any distractions/derailments to come between you and your teen, someone or something else is just waiting to give them the attention and understanding they need. <u>They should have been getting from you</u>. Sex Predators, Gangs, Illegal Drugs, Prescription Drug Addiction, Alcohol, Teen Pregnancy are some of the Danger Zones are just waiting to embrace and take advantage of a teen who needs to be loved, understood, approved, and accepted.

Remember how, when you were a teen, it felt like no one understood you. It felt like you just kept trying to "find yourself" and figure out who you were. You just wanted to figure out where you fit in, what you wanted in life, and what you wanted to do with your life. We just need to be there for our teens and love them while they go through the process. Home needs to be a place where we are always there "For Them". Where—even though we may not always agree with them, we are willing to listen and give them a chance to grow up—without criticizing them, constantly forcing them, or not ever wanting to see it their way. Remember, when they push us away the most, that's when they need us the most.

We need to remind ourselves that our teens will not always think this way. There will be times when your teen will insist something is "Black" just because you said it is "White". There was a time when my children were teens that we could not be in the same room together. I allowed myself to be okay with that. I knew they would grow out of it. I loved them anyway. Yes, today they value that we stuck together and got through it together. My children and grandchildren know I am always there for them and insist on only the best for them, and am constantly praying for their success (God's Best—nothing less for them).

God will help you through this. Ask God daily to give you the wisdom to be an effective parent to your children (and grandparent to your grandchildren) and help you keep a healthy, close relationship going with each of your children in Jesus' name.

List below any areas/situations needing your attention that you have been ignoring or allowing to go on unaddressed.

_____

_____

Ask God to give you the wisdom to know how to effectively take care of that situation and get it back on track. Write down what He tells you here. Continue to pray every day for the wisdom to effectively take care of every situation that comes up in every area of your life and not get derailed ever again. It's one day at a time. You are going to have to realize that derailment issues didn't get like that in a day, and they probably won't snap back into place in a day.

_____

_____

_____

_____

Chapter 24

Spirit of Excellence

Do you find yourself spending more (or all) of your time running after "markets" you haven't yet acquired? While we need to acquire new markets, we must make sure we don't take for granted the customers that we have. We need to make sure they continue to get the personalized customer service and satisfaction they deserve. You must continue to reaffirm and nurture healthy business relationships that have stayed with you through the years. We must not neglect those that have constantly and consistently been loyal through the years. We must remember they have choices too!

There are three primary areas that will keep customers or turn them away. Rate your business on these three (3) aspects:

1. <u>Courtesy</u>

On a recent visit to make the deposit for the business where I work, I drove up to the commercial window and the teller was rude. She was holding a conversation with another person behind the counter in the bank. When I inquired if she was talking to me, she continued to talk to the other person. She finally looked at me, and said, "Now I am talking to you." Even the person she was talking to couldn't believe she had responded to me that way. If that person had only been rude to me once, I could have overlooked it and said maybe she was having a bad day. But this teller was consistently rude to me and other people that had made deposits at that bank. When I mentioned it to another co-worker that had made deposits, she instantly identified and even called that person by name. There is no excuse for rude behavior towards a customer. Excellent customer service should be a way of life, because customers have choices. Daily, our customers pass how many other banks, how many other places that offer the same service to get to yours? Even though I have been loyal to a certain bank, or other business that offers a service I need, I will change when 2 things happen. I will change when 1) the bank begins charging me more than is cost-effective for me to do business with them; or 2) when they become rude or disrespectful to me.

If it were my business, I would change banks. I began driving past the commercial window and choosing the personal banking drive-through window. Those tellers are always cheerful and considerate. They are; however, painfully slow. I can tolerate delays, but I will not tolerate rudeness or disrespect. One day, the teller at the personal banking window asked me where I held my personal banking account. I told her. She asked if I had considered changing to their bank, so I could handle all my banking needs with one stop (offering convenience). I told her that one of the tellers there had been rude to me on several occasions, and that the only reason I visited this bank at all was because my business owner was not open to changing their account elsewhere yet. I also told her they should take lessons from the bank where I do business, because they consistently go out of their way to be cheerful and considerate. I also told her how I appreciate that with every visit my bank offers assistance, solutions and helpfulness—without delays.

2. Quality

Many people have turned away from certain brands of vehicles (some name brands) because the quality in some cases is just not there. This should make the manufacturers more determined to produce a quality product. When compared to some European made models, these vehicles tend to appear disposable, rather than built-to-last. When investing anywhere from $40-80,000 of our hard earned money, we expect to get "built-to-last" reliable transportation—not one that as soon as it is paid off, it falls apart! This holds true on a smaller scale for some appliances, too. We also want vehicles that will hold their resale value once we have driven them off the lot. Why would I want to continue pouring money into something that has no value or cannot hold any value? That's insanity. Business owners will be the first ones to tell you that they wouldn't do that, because business practices like that cause people to lose their businesses. It causes businesses to go bankrupt. However, some auto-makers and appliance manufacturers expect us to do it every day. Buyers beware.

3. Excellent Customer Service

When was the last time you as a business owner, or person dealing with the public, asked your customer(s): "How can I help you today? Have I answered all your questions? Has your customer service today been what you needed?" "If there is anything else I can help you with, just call or email me at_____. When a customer feels they have been helped and received the assistance/service they went to your business to get either through a phone call or visit, they not only will leave satisfied, they will tell others about their satisfactory experience. They will return for more of the same level and quality of service.

On the other hand, when a customer feels they have NOT been helped or received the assistance/service they went to your business to get either through a phone call or visit, they not only leave dissatisfied and disgruntled, they will tell many others about their dissatisfactory experience, and not ever return for more of the same dissatisfaction and lack of quality or lack of service. Each time you "go the extra mile" or "go above and beyond the call of duty", your service will not go unrewarded.

On a recent trip to a world renowned resort theme park, I had several very disappointing experiences. In the past, this legend had prided themselves in excellent customer service—even to the point of teaching other major corporations "how excellent customer service is done". A large number of people around me were also disappointed. They walked away from the restaurant where we were without paying for their food. <u>They stood in line to complain to the restaurant manager</u>. Some of them were livid, because they had to wait so long to get served even though they had reservations, and other people who walked in after them had gotten served first. The food was unacceptable. It was cold or the order was wrong. Not wanting to spend more than an hour in the restaurant, I began to walk to the desk to ask for my check. The waitress came to me to ask why I was leaving. I said I needed to pay for my meal so I could return to the park and use my time enjoying the rides and attractions. She thought I was trying to leave without paying for my meal. I assured her that I wanted to pay, so I could leave. She informed me that every time a customer left without paying for their meal, she had to pay out of her pocket for that group's meal. She said in her area alone, there were 15 groups that had left that day without paying.

Needless to say, there was NO excellent customer service going on there.

Consistent courtesy, quality, and excellent customer service—these are integral (must have) ingredients in the anatomy of any successful business. We need to remember to always include them in every aspect of our jobs, every day. These factors make a difference. These are absolute factors in "earning your customer's business". These 3 will attract new customers, sustain business levels and sales during uncertain economic times, and retain the health of your product, the health of your business, and retain your clientele.

Think about it. People every day leave perfectly good food sitting in their pantries, refrigerators and freezers at home to go get restaurant food if there is courtesy, quality and excellent customer service waiting for them once they get there. People every day leave perfectly good clothing sitting in their closets at home to go shopping at the Mall and get more of the latest fashion if there is courtesy, quality and excellent customer service waiting for them once they get there. People every day leave perfectly good shelter at home or at their apartment to vacation or get away to a hotel room, condo or cabin if there is courtesy, quality and excellent customer service waiting for them once they get there.

If you had to rate your business (as a business owner), how would you rate your business in the areas of:
(5 = Highest, 1 = Lowest)

Courtesy _____, Quality _____, Excellent Customer Service _____

If you had to rate your job (as an employee), how would you rate your department and/or your position in the areas of:
(5 = Highest, 1 = Lowest)

Courtesy _____, Quality _____, Excellent Customer Service _____

Think about areas of your business or your job that came to mind as you were reading the chapter on "Have You Earned Their Business Lately?"

Were there any Courtesy, Quality or Excellent Customer Service experiences or issues that came to mind?

List them here.

Courtesy: _____

Quality: _____

Excellent Customer Service: _____

What can you do to make sure these areas come up to a higher standard?

Courtesy: _____

Quality: _____

Excellent Customer Service: _____

<u>Pray this Prayer</u>: Lord God, show me any areas that are lacking in Courtesy, Quality, or Customer service in my business, my department, and my job. Show me what you would have me to do to bring them up to the higher standard which will cause me in my position (my job), my department, and my business to experience higher levels of success in Jesus' name.

_____

_____

Part Four

Living The Best You've Ever Lived

*RIP Away Limitations,
Experience Higher Levels of Success!*

Chapter 25

Resist

Remember when R.I.P. used to imply "Rest In Peace". Well, it's a new day. R.I.P. now implies Resist, Insist, Persist......so you can live the best you've ever lived! You need to RIP away any limitations. Rip as in tearing away and discarding—never to allow in your life again. As you continually do this, you are not going backward—only moving forward. You are gaining ground, completing projects, attaining accomplishments, and reaching higher levels of success in your life and reaching your destiny!

In the pages to follow, you will see how God's best (His Word) works for you 24/7. When you are awake it is working, and when you are asleep—it is working. God's Word is <u>working out everything for your good</u>. **Romans 8:28** *And we know that ALL things work together for good to them that love God, to them who are the called according to His purpose*. The world looks for such investments…in all the wrong places. In the previous chapters, God has shown you ten reasons people and businesses fail, how to position yourself for success (overcoming all limitations), how to ward off hindrances and hold on to your success.

Now it's time to employ (put it to work for you) a method that gets results for the rest of YOUR unlimited, cannot be contained, "God's got so much more in store" successful (<u>FULL OF SUCCESS</u>) life!

The nuggets contained in these pages are so powerful, so unlimiting, so unshackling, so propelling, that when you put them into motion and begin working them in your life, you will see RESULTS. However, God wants me to warn you. If you don't <u>Resist</u> the following 3 pitfalls, they will 1) suck you down, 2) hold you down, and 3) keep you under.

<u>Come Out of Your Lo Debar</u>

Come out of your Lo Debar. For those of you who haven't heard or know nothing about Lo Debar, it's time to not only get understanding about where (and what) Lo Debar is, but to stay away from it. Lo Debar is your lowest place, your dry place, a place where nothing works, and you hide from the very situation that can be effective, cause you to attain your goals, and release your success. Lo Debar is Intimidation, Humiliation or Dread. Lo Debar keeps you down, keeps you under, and makes you wish you were dead. Lo Debar is the lowest place you've ever been—mentally, emotionally, physically, and financially. Lo Debar is when you hit the lowest of the lows. You feel like everybody and everything is laughing at you. You say to yourself, "How can I ever face my peers, neighbors, co-workers, church or family members again?"

Resist the urge to live below what God said you could live Resist living below the promises He said you could have. Resist the urge to allow your life to be dictated by this person or that person's opinion, haughtiness and arrogance. Do not allow your level of success and achievement to be measured by someone that is not going where you are going, Someone who doesn't have near the backbone, character or integrity in their little finger that you have in your whole body—because greater is He that is in you, than He that is in the world. **1 John 4:4** *Ye are of God, little children, and have overcome them: because greater is He that is in you, that he that is in the world.*

You <u>have to</u> get past the opinions of men (and women). Do not allow yourself to be bothered by those who look down their noses at you. Those who are critical and faultfinding of you. Those who can only feel good about themselves once they put someone else down. Those snobs who snub you and want to make you feel like you don't belong—and never will. Those bullies and snobs who harass you and treat you like dirt and "dog you" (harass you) so that you don't want to go to school or work anymore. Resist that. Resist comparing yourself with individuals or groups that think or behave that way. Resist trying to meet their approval or live according to their standards. God's approval is the only approval you have to meet. God's standards are above every other standard, and the only standard you have to keep. **Isaiah 59:19** *So shall they fear the name of the Lord from the west, and His glory from the rising of the sun. When the enemy shall come in like a flood, the Spirit of the Lord shall lift up a standard against him.* God will not allow His children to be bullied! God's word clearly states that when the enemy (bully, accuser of the brethren, harasser) comes in---------then, like a flood the Spirit of the Lord (the presence and power of Almighty God) will lift up a standard against him (and those who have allowed themselves to be used by him to come against you). **Jeremiah 1:8** *Be not afraid of their faces: for I am with thee to deliver thee, saith the Lord.*

Resist comparing yourself with others. That's an unhealthy comparison. Resist thinking that you will "get to the top or have the advantage" if you get in good with the boss. Promotion comes from God. **Psalms 75:6-7** *For promotion (exaltation) cometh neither from the east, nor from the west, nor from the south. 7) But God is the judge: He putteth down one, and setteth up another.*

As you were reading about Lo Debar, what "dry places" have you been going through that came to mind? What "dry places" have you gotten "stuck in"? Think about it. "Dry places" where there is no increase, no promotion or place for advancement. Write them here.

Mentally: _____

Emotionally: _____

Physically: _____

Financially: _____

Stagnation: _____

Now, we know that God is a God of results, increase, multiplication and success. Say this prayer: "Lord God, I pray that you would show me the place where you want me to be and cause me to come out of my Lo Debar (dry places) right now. Move the things that have blocked me in the past and cause me to get to my wealthy place, my place of promotion, my place of increase and success (mentally, emotionally, physically, financially, next level assignment) in Jesus' name".

Resist Being Average

Average people don't make a difference. Average people don't get remembered for making an impact. Average people only do what they absolutely have to in order to get by in life. Average people don't have any ambition. Average people don't see any need to get ahead or improve themselves. Average is a mindset. Dictionary.com defines [14]average as: insignificant, lacking quality, lacking distinction, common and ordinary. Successful people eliminate average mindsets from their thinking. In order to finish our projects, reach our goals and accomplishments, and be truly successful, we have to press past average into a mindset of excellence. Excellence is going the "extra mile" (doing more than what's expected of you)—even when no one is watching. Excellence is doing what is right even though it's not popular or convenient. People remember excellence. Excellence stands out in a group or department. Why do you think employers have "Employee of the Month" and "Employee of the Year" awards? These awards are designed to reward "above average" service on the job, "above average" customer service, "above average" production, a person who consistently goes above and beyond the call of duty to get the job done.

Average people don't mind doing things the way they've always been done and aren't open to new ways of doing things. Average people don't want to change or try new things and broaden their horizons. Average people don't want to overcome their limitations; they just take the path that's easiest and settle for what life hands them. Average people don't want to come out of their comfort zones. Average people always gravitate to "what happened in the past", and "this is how we've always done it before", because they want to stay with what's familiar.

Average people don't succeed and they certainly don't impress others to want to follow them. Why would God want to entrust (bless and bestow) increase on someone who is not willing to do more than the bare minimum (only what they absolutely have to) in order to get by in life?

As you were reading the "Resist Being Average" section, what areas of your life, your business, your wife (or husband's life) or your children's lives came to mind? In what area or situation have you settled for "average"? List it here.

_____

_____

_____

_____

You must also ask yourself, "<u>When</u> did I become average-minded in that area?" Another valid question for your business, spouse, or children would be, "When did that department I manage, that department I am in, my marriage, that area of my child's academics, or the planning and positioning for my child's career and future become average". Note when it took place.

Think about this. Because "average" is a mindset, ask yourself, "Did I become average-minded because I was raised with that example and in that environment?" Which, incidentally—is not an excuse for being average, because you do not have to become a product of your environment. You do not have to remain a product of your environment. <u>You have to choose not to stay that way</u>.

Average mindsets have a way of subtly creeping in on you, then becoming a way of life. You don't want to reach farther, climb higher, go to the next level of success. Once you realize (identify) any area of your life or business that has gone into "Average Mode", you need to shift gears and get going again. Yes, I'm going to point you to the tortoise and the hare again. That Hare got "Average-minded" in the middle of his race. The finish line, the goal, the completion of the assignment, overcoming that limitation, having success and reaching his destiny wasn't important—it lost importance along the way. He lost his momentum, his priorities got out of order, his life, his journey; his destiny got put "on hold" indefinitely because he became average-minded.

<u>**Ephesians 5:14**</u> *Wherefore He saith, Awake thou that sleepest, and arise from the dead, and Christ shall give thee light*. Average-minded people have been lulled into unconsciousness (sleep) by that way of thinking. They fall

into a rut of going to work at that minimum wage job, coming home, seeing about the children, doing homework, getting baths, going to bed, then doing it all again. There's so much more Christ has in store for you! When you become average-minded, your ambition (willingness to do what it takes to get there) has gone to sleep like the Hare, and your business, your dreams and your destiny are in danger of dying.

In order to "Resist Being Average", identify <u>how</u> you, your business, that department you are in, your spouse, and any areas in your children's academics or positioning for their careers and future became average. List here how it became "average".

_____

_____

_____

_____

    In Ephesians 5:14 above, it clearly states that we are to first wake up to the fact (identify) that we have become "average-minded". Identify when and how it got there, then ask God to give thee light (understanding and a path forward), so now we operate in forward thinking—not average-minded thinking.

    To "Resist Being Average-Minded" we pray, "Lord God, help me to see clearly any areas of my life, my business, my marriage, and my children's academics and positioning for their careers and future that have "become average", in Jesus' name. Show me (enlighten me about) what I must do and what must be done daily to "Resist Being Average" and to position myself, my business, my marriage, and my children for increase, promotion, advancement, and reaching our destiny, in Jesus' name."

Chapter 26

Insist

Insist on the best that God has for you, your business and your family. ONLY success is God's best—not 2nd best. No compromise. Not what the world calls "the best", what God's word says you can and will have. Nothing less than the best. It's called the promises of God. I don't know about you, but if God says I can have it, then I want it. I don't just want it on Sundays and Wednesdays, I want it 24/7/365. And I don't just want a little bit, <u>I want it ALL</u>.

When my daughter was about 4 years old, she and her Daddy went on an outing to the country store. It was always his habit to buy a candy bar or treat of her choice for her when she would go the store with him. When they would get to the store, he would tell her, "Get what you want, Baby". (He would call her Baby). Her reply would always be, "Back up the truck, Daddy". When Daddy God tells you in His word all the things you can have, don't ask or settle for just a little bit. <u>I want it ALL</u>. I call God "Daddy God", because it says in the Bible we are to call him "Abba Father". We are supposed to have that kind of relationship with Him!

In the example that follows, you will see how God expects us to insist on great things—insist on ALL of it, not some of it. We are to insist on total victory, not a partial bypass—or a glimpse of God's glory. We are to have total healing, total victory, total increase (mega increase), total accomplishment and complete fulfillment of the visions and dreams He gives us. We limit God by thinking He is as small and limited as our thinking (our view of any given situation). Instead, we are to insist on higher levels of success in our lives by asking God help us to see things as He sees them. We are to ask God to help us understand things the way He understands them. We are to ask God to enlarge our territory, and receive the increase He always intended us to live and operate in, so that we don't go through life missing it. We don't serve a "barely-getting-by" God. We are to ask God that He causes us to see with the eyes of Christ. When we begin seeing (understanding) things the way God sees them, we will not ever want to live below the standards, the provisions, the potential, and the status that God said we could have.

2 Kings 13:18-19 *And he said, Take the arrows. And he took them. And he said unto the king of Israel, Smite (strike) upon the ground. And he smote thrice, and stayed (stopped). 19) And the man of God was wroth with him, and said, Thou shouldest have smitten five or six times; then hadst thou smitten Syria till thou hadst consumed (destroyed) it: whereas now thou shalt smite Syria but thrice.*

What the prophet Elisha is pointing out here, is that the king should have aimed high, and asked for total victory. Instead, he only shot a meager 3 times. Isn't your marriage worth it? How about the future of your children? Don't you want to see them succeed and prosper in their careers and in their families? How about your health and well-being (wholeness)? When we pray, we are to ask God for ALL He said we could have, not a smidgen. **Ephesians 3:20-21** *Now unto Him that is able to do exceeding abundantly above all that we ask or think, according to the power that worketh in us, 21) Unto Him be glory in the church by Christ Jesus throughout all ages, world without end. Amen.* He already pointed out in Ephesians 3:20-21 that He is able to do exceedingly abundantly above (so much more that we cannot fathom it) what we will ever ask or imagine (think of to ask) of Him.

Because He is not a man that he should lie, <u>I believe He will do whatever He says in His word He will do</u>. <u>I believe that I can have whatever He says I can have</u>. That's the kind of belief, confidence (faith) we must have in God in order to walk in the success levels He predestined for us. **Mark 11:24** *Therefore I say unto you, What things soever ye desire, when ye pray, believe that ye receive them, and ye shall have them.*

God said we are to have an abundant life. **John 10:10** *The thief cometh not, but for to steal, and to kill, and to destroy: I am come that they might have life, and that they might have it more abundantly.* We are to insist on an abundant life and not settle for anything less—in any area of our lives (our health), our businesses, our goals, projects, academics, finances, and levels of success. If you never saw it (understood it) that way before, it's time to start living it now!

Insist on having <u>EVERYTHING God said you could have</u>—not what man said you could or couldn't have. To some of us, obstacles are growing up with sickness or disease. Some of you reading this book right now, the doctors have said "they will never walk again, talk again, have movement of certain limbs again, or drive a car again". RIP away the limitations and have what God said you could have. To some of us, it was the environment we grew up in. We grew up "on the wrong side of the tracks". We grew up in the projects. We grew up in the south. We grew up in a home where they didn't believe in this or that about the truths of God. We grew up in a home where someone was always telling you, "You'll never amount to anything" and "you don't know nothing, you're just a dumb kid". We grew up with some relative telling us "you're dreaming, you better wake up to reality" (trying to kill our dreams and creativity). We grew up with parents that had no ambition — so we grew up with the example of not ever reaching for better than what life handed us. We grew up watching our parent(s) allowing that government check that comes in the mail every month to dictate to us what we could buy, dictate to you what you can have in life, and dictate what level of success you are going to live in. We grew up with "that's the way Grandma and Grandpa did it — and they got along just fine (had a pretty good life), that's how I'm going to do it. Oh, My God.

If that was you, that's not God's best. You don't have to be a product of your environment. You can and you must come out of "your environment" — where you came from and the way you were raised. God has so much more in store for you, but you have to come out from your past and reach for everything He said you could have. You have to INSIST on YOU walking in the levels of accomplishment, achievement, and success that God said you would walk in — not what the world said, or what the Television said, or what the teacher that labeled you said, or what any man (or woman) said about you (if it was not in line with the word of God). Any woman that has been verbally abused has been held down by her environment. Any child that has been verbally abused has been held down by their environment. Insist on God's best and stop settling for what man is telling you. When you realize that God's word IS THE FINAL AUTHORITY on everything, you will stop settling for what man tells you that you can have.

When you are paying for a service and you are not getting that service, don't you get frustrated and upset? When your satellite signal or cable service goes out, don't you get frustrated and upset? When you go on vacation and stay in a hotel, if your room is not clean, don't you get frustrated and upset? You are entitled. As a child of God, you are entitled to certain things. You are entitled to certain privileges, certain standards, certain lifestyle and freedoms, and certain successes. Any time you don't operate (walk) in them on a daily basis, it is the same thing as not getting a service you are entitled to. You didn't pay for it; Jesus paid the price for it. You are now doing yourself a disservice (cheating yourself) by not walking in it. I'm sure that God in His panoramic view of things is wondering "Why are they not enjoying and attaining ALL the entitlements that have been placed at their disposal, when my precious son, Jesus, paid the ultimate price so they could have it ALL. <u>Why</u>?" Now you need to ask yourself, "Why?" It's called unused, untapped, (wasted) forfeited potential. Not so different from a child or young adult who died at an early age. They certainly never lived out their potential. That's not cold, that's the truth. That's what gets parents, friends and relatives angry. That's what saddens God deeply.

Instead of INSISTING on being all God said you could be, and INSISTING on all God said you could do, you live your life with marginal or minimal goals, marginal or minimal accomplishments, marginal or minimal dreams, marginal or minimal levels of success. God's got so much more in store for you, your business, your family, your children and grandchildren. You have to INSIST.

Throughout the Bible, there are examples of people who insisted on having what God said they could have. **Luke 18:2-8** *Saying, There was in a city a judge, which feared not God, neither regarded man: 3) And there was a widow in that city; and she came unto him, saying, Avenge me of mine adversary (make it right, give me what is rightfully mine). 4) And he would not for a while: but afterward he said within himself, Though I fear not God, nor regard man; 5) Yet because this widow troubleth me, I will avenge her, lest by her continual coming she weary me. 6) And the Lord said, Hear what the unjust judge saith. 7) And shall not God avenge his own elect, which cry day and night unto Him, though He bear long with them? 8) I tell you that He will avenge them speedily. Nevertheless when the Son of man cometh, shall he find faith on the earth?* This woman kept insisting that the judge (even though he didn't fear God or care about anyone else except himself) needed to make it right and give her what was rightfully hers. Because of her insistence, he awarded her request.

The Shunammite woman went to Elijah when her son got sick and insisted that he make him well. She vowed not to leave Elijah's side until the child recovered. **2 Kings 4:30** *And the mother of the child said, As the Lord liveth, and as thy soul liveth, I will not leave thee, And he arose, and followed her (so she could direct Elijah to where* *her son lay dead).* Because of her insistence, this woman received her son back from the dead!

Jacob wrestled the angel and would not let him go until he blessed him. **Genesis 32:26** *And he said, Let me go, for the day breaketh. And he said, I will not let thee go, except thou bless me.* Jacob insisted on his blessing—even though it cost him to walk with a limp the rest of his life.

When Lazarus died, Jesus went to see about him after about 4 days. This is the ultimate situation of insistence. Jesus insisted that Lazarus come back from the dead—instead of leaving him in the tomb. Lazarus obviously had not finished his work on this earth! **John 11:43-44** *And when He thus had spoken, He cried with a loud voice, Lazarus, come forth. 44) And he that was dead came forth, bound hand and foot with graveclothes: and his face was bound about with a napkin. Jesus saith unto them, Loose him, and let him go.*

Think about it. What area(s) of your business, your personal life, your marriage, your children or grandchildren's lives seem to have gone so far out of whack—gone into a downward spiral? Perhaps they will need your help. Pick up the phone, text or email them insisting that they cry out to God to bless them, fix that situation, it's turnaround time—it's their turn. God is a God of <u>ALL THINGS ARE POSSIBLE</u>. **Matthew 19:26** *But Jesus beheld them, and said unto them, With men this is impossible; but with God all things are possible.* Maybe in the past, these same situations, and these same people in your life have turned their back on you, vented at you, remained in denial that this or that was not going on—instead of insisting on getting the help they desperately need.

First, let's list those areas and situations here.

_____

_____

_____

_____

_____

Now, you need to pray the Prayer of Insistence: Lord God, I bring to you _____ (name the person and situation with specifics in place). Even though this situation seems to be impossible according to man, I know that you can and will divinely intervene and overrule and overtake the natural course of events and turn this person and situation around for your glory and their good. So, I place _____ (person and situation with specifics in place) in Your most capable hands. I am looking to you and requesting this from you—not anyone else. I am leaving it with you because You are the only one who can do it. If you don't do it, it won't be done. I command _____ (name) and _____ (situation) to line up with your word in Jesus' name. According to Matthew 19:26 this situation IS POSSIBLE with YOU. As a child of God, I insist on having what You said I could have and _____ (name that person/situation) having what You said they could have. We will not be denied. It shall come to pass, in Jesus' name.

1 John 5:14-15 *And this is the confidence that we have in Him, that, if we ask ANY THING according to His will, He heareth us: 15) And if we know that He hear us, whatsoever we ask, we KNOW THAT WE HAVE the petitions that we desired (asked) of Him.*

Chapter 27

Persist

All my life I have experienced obstacles popping up in front of me. I could list them here, but the main thing is that I did not let them stop me. I went to God and asked Him to show me (direct me) enlighten me (reveal to me) — because He is the only one who knows what's best for me NOW and in the future. Remember, He alone has the panoramic view. He is my "I.T. Guy" — my "Go-To" Person. Yes, He alone has ALL the Information, ALL the Insight, and ALL the Issue resolution (answers) I will ever need — because He always knows what is causing the situation, I don't. Isn't that what you rely on your "I.T. Guy" for? Some people refer to these as "Technical Support Experts". Still, when you don't have the service you need, can't get your work done, can't meet the deadline (the need), and your job (or your life — possibly the life of a loved one) depends on it... When you don't have the answer(s), your life and any forms of progress — even the very breath in your body, can come to a screeching halt.

Isaiah 48:17-18 *This is what the Lord says—your Redeemer, the Holy One of Israel; "I am the Lord your God, who teaches you what is best for you, who directs you in the way you should go. 18) <u>If only you had paid attention to my commands</u>...."*

God clearly states in His word that He alone teaches us what is best for us and directs us in the way we should go <u>at all times</u>. Our part is to look to him, listen for our instructions, and obey (follow) the instructions once we receive them. Upon obeying the instructions we receive from Him in <u>every situation</u>, we will have SUCCESS, HEALTH, and PEACE. Think about it. EVERTHING in life hedges on SUCCESS, HEALTH and PEACE.

If you don't have health and peace, you cannot attain success—you can't even enjoy it even if you attain it. We need to seek God in every situation, every decision, every day—or we will play hit and miss with everything in life. There will be CERTAIN mistakes, CERTAIN wasted time, CERTAIN wasted effort, CERTAIN wasted energy, CERTAIN wasted money. It's called LOSS and FAILURE. At that point, we have played into the enemy's plan (he comes with the sole intent and assignment to KILL, STEAL, and DESTROY). We become an easy target, a mullet—due to our disobedience.

Hebrews 10:38 *The just shall live by the Word of God.*

The Word of God is the final authority in EVERY situation, decision, and experience in your life. Whenever you use the Word of God as the standard in your situation, use the Word of God as the standard in making your decision, use the Word of God as the standard for your way of thinking, use the Word of God for your standard in the way you look at things, it becomes the final authority and CANNOT FAIL.

We are to "keep on keeping on". Every day, we are to make a step in a progressive direction—in every area of our lives. We are to keep our momentum going. We are to consistently and constantly keep going. We should always be working on something progressive. Every day, we should RIP the limitations away (Resist, Insist, and Persist) and walk in the next level of success that God has for us for each new day.

Hebrews 12:1 *Wherefore seeing we also are compassed about with so great a cloud of witnesses, let us <u>lay aside every weight</u> (every obstacle and limitation), <u>and the sin</u> (whatever mindset or lifestyle that doesn't line up with the Word of God) <u>which doth so easily beset us</u>, and let us run with patience the race that is set before us.*

As you were reading the pages of this book, I pray that the truths included herein challenged you to identify and correct your limitations, seek and obey God's wisdom to overcome them, and attain higher levels of success in your life!

For More Information
Concerning Motivational Seminars and
Speaking Engagements For
Your Business, Church or Civic Group

Contact:

Email: Lona@highersuccesstoday.com

For Higher Levels of Success In Your Life!

Endnotes

All definitions were taken from Dictionary.com and are cited below. All defined words are listed here, and the citations are the same for each word.

Words defined (in order of appearance):

[1] Procrastination
[2] Murmuring
[3] Complaining
[4] Waste
[5] Invest
[6] Destroy
[7] Double-minded
[8] Instability
[9] Greed
[10] Enticed
[11] Clutter
[12] Confusion
[13] Derailment
[14] Average

American Psychological Association (APA):
> procrastination. (n.d.). *Online Etymology Dictionary*. Retrieved March 1, 2011, from Dictionary.com website: http://dictionary.reference.com/browse/procrastination

Chicago Manual Style (CMS):
> procrastination. Dictionary.com. *Online Etymology Dictionary*. Douglas Harper, Historian. http://dictionary.reference.com/browse/procrastination (accessed: March 1, 2011).

Modern Language Association (MLA):
> "procrastination." *Online Etymology Dictionary*. Douglas Harper, Historian. 1 Mar. 2011. <Dictionary.com http://dictionary.reference.com/browse/procrastination>.

Institute of Electrical and Electronics Engineers (IEEE):
> Dictionary.com, "procrastination," in *Online Etymology Dictionary*. Source location: Douglas Harper, Historian. http://dictionary.reference.com/browse/

procrastination. Available: http://dictionary.reference.com. Accessed: March 1, 2011.

BibTeX Bibliography Style (BibTeX)
@article {Dictionary.com2011,
   title = {Online Etymology Dictionary},
   month = {Mar},
   day = {1},
   year = {2011},
   url = {http://dictionary.reference.com/browse/procrastination}

Research Reference employed: Strong's Exhaustive Concordance of the Bible by James Strong, S.T.D., LL.D. published by Macdonald Publishing Company, McLean, VA 22102